# Snapshots!
## Educational Insights from the Thornburg Center

Edited by Sara Armstrong, Ph.D.

Armstrong, Sara, editor
Snapshots!
Educational Insights from the Thornburg Center

ISBN 0-942207-16-5 (pbk.)
Copyright, ©, 2003 by the respective authors

Published in the United States of America.

ISBN 0-942207-16-5

The authors of this book can be contacted at:
Thornburg Center
847-277-7691

TCPD2020@aol.com
http://www.tcpd.org

# Contents

# Foreword

The Thornburg Center is an affiliation of world-class thinkers and practitioners in the field of education. While much of our work is devoted to thinking deeply about the most effective ways technology can be used in support of learners and educators alike, we are not technologists. What unites us is our deep caring for children and for the institutions and communities that prepare young people for their future.

When I first started the Center in 1981, personal computers were in their infancy. Even so, battle lines were being drawn between those who would use these tools for decontextualized drill and those who adopted a more constructivist approach to their thinking. It quickly became apparent that (as a member of an apparent minority in the constructivist camp) there were other kindred spirits whose enthusiasm and depth of caring was as great, if not greater, than mine. Person by person, step by step, the Thornburg Center started to grow, reaching the point today of being home to some of the finest educational thinkers in the world.

Members of the Center have many perspectives, making our internal meetings quite spirited. We embrace the adage that those who all think alike do not think very much. But while we may look at the jewel of education through different facets, we are all focused on its center: the heart and mind of the learner, and the heart and mind of the teachers who dedicate themselves to preparing the future leaders of our world.

This modest volume provides an opportunity for you to experience insights of each member of the Center. Each author reflects on a topic of current interest, so these chapters can be read in any order. They are arranged alphabetically by author.

As I read each of the following essays for the first time, I reflected on how talented this group is. Each associate is passionate about working with educators in any setting to help insure that teachers have the resources they need to do their heart's work most effectively. Toward that end, you'll find Thornburg Center associates presenting at most major educational conferences both in the United States and elsewhere. (Any of them can be contacted by e-mailing them through the Center at tcpd2020@aol.com) The following brief biographical sketches illustrate some of the depth found in this organization:

**Sara Armstrong, Ph.D.:** Storyteller, pedagogical expert, and proponent of creative uses of technology with young people, Dr. Armstrong draws on her 30 years of experience in education to inspire audiences, develop and implement professional development, and advance district and statewide systemic change.

**Bonnie Bracey**: Bonnie is a teacher-agent of change, and a mentor teacher who works nationally and internationally with technology integration projects that emphasize the use of technology as media. She was the only classroom teacher appointed by President Clinton to the National Information Infrastructure Advisory Council, and served as an instructor in the Clinton administration's CyberED initiative. A former Fulbright Exchange Teacher in India and elementary school teacher in Virginia, Ms. Bracey was selected as a Christa McAuliffe Educator by the National Education Association. She is also recognized as an expert on the topic of the digital divide and addressing such inequities.

6

**Lynell Burmark, Ph.D.**: A distinguished pioneer in education, Lynell has worked as a teacher – with years of classroom teaching experience in both K-12 and higher education – as an administrator, and as a professional speaker. She is also co-founder of VisionShift International, an organization dedicated to advancing innovative new approaches to learning.

**Lou Fournier**: With a distinguished career as an author, composer, and presenter, Lou is frequently requested to speak on the fields of humor, creativity, stress abatement, and purposeful uses of music. He is the author of several books, including *Enlighten Up!* (with Lynell Burmark), ASCD, 2003; *What's So Funny About Education*, Corwin, 2003; and *Power & Purpose*, Lou Fournier Marzeles, 2003. His recent CDs, *In a Heartbeat* and *Enlighten Up*, are also available.

**Ted McCain**: Ted is an internationally recognized author, futurist, speaker, and educator. He has been an education administrative assistant, technology consultant, and teacher, and is currently the Coordinator of Instructional Technology at Maple Ridge Secondary School in Vancouver, B.C. Ted is also a recipient of the prestigious Prime Minister's Award for Teaching Excellence.

**Bernajean Porter**: Bernajean specializes in organizational change. She uses the application of systems thinking and chaos theory to deal with the challenges of change, planning and re-culturing efforts in education today. Bernajean facilitates future searches, community meetings, consensus building, conflict resolutions, creating change cultures, designing effective staff development programs and district leadership skills for involving large groups in decision-making and accountability. She is author of *Grappling with Accountability 2002: MAPPing Tools for Organizing and Assessing Technology for Student Results; Evaluating Student Computer-based*

*Products: Training and Resources Tools for Using Scoring Guides;* and *Nutz and Boltz for Engaging Large Groups.*


**Ferdi Serim**: Ferdi helps people learn to read, write and think, using technology to expand the boundaries of what they read, write and think about. His work as an Associate of the Thornburg Center, board member of the Consortium for School Networking (CoSN), director of the Online Internet Institute (OII), and jazz musician helps people understand and harness technology's transforming potentials for distributed learning and networked knowing. He is the author of *NetLearning: Why Teachers Use the Internet* (published by Songline, a division of O'Reilly and Associates), *From Computers to Community: Unlocking the Potentials of the Wired Classroom* (published by Centrinity, inc) and *Information Technology for Learning: No School Left Behind* (by Big6 Associates).


**Gary Stager**: For 20 years, Gary has helped learners of all ages embrace the power of computers as intellectual laboratories and vehicles for self-expression. He led professional development in the world's first laptop schools, designed online graduate school programs and is a collaborator in the MIT Media Lab's Future of Learning Group.


**David D. Thornburg, Ph.D.**: The founder and Director of Global Operations for the Thornburg Center, David is the author of numerous books on education and technology, is a respected commentator for PBS, is a popular international speaker and workshop presenter, and tireless advocate for an educational system that honors the integrity and creativity of students and teachers alike. David has received numerous awards for his work and is considered one of the top presenters in the field of education and technology in the world.

(You can learn more about any of these people, at the Thornburg Center Web site at http://www.tcpd.org)

As impressive as their credentials are, the true value of these people is found in the ideas they share with you on the following pages.

David Thornburg

Lake Barrington, Illinois

June, 2003

# The Power of Storytelling in Education

Sara Armstrong, Ph.D.
tcpd2020@aol.com

*I will tell you something about stories,*
*They aren't just entertainment.*
*Don't be fooled.*
*They are all we have, you see,*
*all we have to fight off*
*illness and death. ...*

*– Leslie Silko, Ceremony*

## Foundations of Thinking, Bases of Interactions

One of the most memorable experiences of my first year in teaching - more than 30 years ago -was an afternoon spent in a Montessori preschool classroom, where the five year olds were composing

11

stories with movable alphabet letters on rugs on the floor while the younger children napped.

Maria Montessori, Italian doctor and gifted educator, observed the enormous propensity toward language inherent in human beings, and most evident in children from birth to six years old. This "sensitive period" for language manifests itself in young children in a variety of ways, including a keen interest in learning to understand and speak the language(s) they hear, trying to interpret text wherever they encounter it (*e.g.*, in storybooks being read to them, on signs and billboards in their environment, on TV, etc.), and sharing their own experiences with others through writing. (In the Montessori language program, writing is emphasized before reading, because the stories each of us has to tell will always be more immediate, more important, more vital than anything others have written for us to read.)

Teacher education programs help students understand four parts of language arts: listening, speaking, writing, reading. Doctors tell us that the sense of hearing is the first we acquire as a developing fetus, and the last we lose as we finish our days on Earth. Making sounds - and moving as quickly as possible to making coherent sounds, so we can get our needs met - is also an early acquisition, and one we refine all our lives. Since human beings are social animals, that is, it is of primary importance that each of us participates in meaningful ways with someone or ones for survival, clear communication through speech is an extremely important attribute.

Children come to school well-versed in listening and speaking, and our educational system is built on the assumption that these abilities can be exploited and expanded, and here's where writing and reading come into play as extensions of our physical abilities of hearing and speech. While technically not necessary for survival in

12

the strictest sense, writing and reading allow us to transcend time and space for purposes of deepening our own understanding of self and our current and future place in the world in which we live.

The way we do this is through sharing our stories. By "story," I mean an offering through words (written or spoken) that conveys personal information about an experience.

Roger Schank, known for his work in artificial intelligence, comments, "Our knowledge of the world is more or less equivalent to the set of experiences that we have had, but our communication is limited by the number of stories we know to tell. In other words, all we have are experiences, but all we can effectively tell others are stories. ... Communication consists of selecting stories that we know and telling them to others at the right time. Learning from one's own experiences depends upon being able to communicate our experiences as stories to others."

Schank's ideas are key to the educational enterprise. Stories can only be told if we have made meaning out of an experience. Learning in many curricular areas can only be demonstrated by the telling of stories - the communicating of understanding of information that has made up an experience, that is, learning the content.

Stories are shared for many reasons. Included among them are establishing each of us as individuals with a unique set of experiences, indicating what is of importance to us so that we can compare our experiences with others in order to deepen our own or others', providing new information to others to get new information back, and checking for our own understanding.

Stories are more than requests or statements. They are often described as having a beginning, middle, and an end. This structure indicates that an event or experience has been thought about, taken beyond the original event or experience, and offered in a specific context. There is conscious thought involved; some reflection has taken place, for this story to be offered at this specific time in this situation.

## The Power of Stories

As I walked around that Montessori classroom I mentioned earlier, I noticed one small child deeply engrossed in placing the small, wooden movable alphabet letters carefully in word groups on his rug. For an hour at least, he silently laid out the letters to recreate his thoughts. Finally finished, he ran to me, grabbed my hand, and led me over to his rug. Duly impressed, I asked him if we should read what he had written out loud together. And here's where he amazed me. He said, "No." For him, the act of creation, the first step in communication - getting the words out from inside himself into a form he already knew was going to let me understand him - was what the afternoon was about. Later, being assured that I understood what he meant in his words by reading and talking about them would become important. But that day, getting thought into words was primary. Montessori was brilliant: Writing before reading - then reading has a purpose!

The journey of children from listening to speaking and writing is reflected in the historical availability of stories, and their power. Jane Yolen, noted author of books for children and adults, says, "If the oral tradition came first, the second type of [written] tale came hard on its heels. Once writing was established, the written word worked its own magic on the world of story. ...Not only listeners seated in a particular audience at a particular time could hear the

14

tale. Audiences separated by time and space could hear it as well. Authority is a word that grew from the root author. And so author and power became inextricably linked." (2000)

I believe the power Yolen speaks of can be characterized by the importance of one's own experiences communicated through one's unique voice. Helping children tell their stories, through a variety of means and media, to a variety of audiences, is the most important thing teachers do.

Al Rogers and Yvonne Andrés, pioneers in telecommunications in the classroom, still promote broadening the audience for student work as much as possible. They found, through their own experiences and feedback over many years from teachers who have participated in online shared learning projects (Global SchoolNet: http://www.gsn.org), that students work very hard when they know their work will be shared broadly. When the audience for a student's writing, multimedia project, or presentation is more than a single teacher, the student accepts and responds to accountability requirements. Students take seriously what they have said when they get responses from younger (or older) children at their school, or from distant, perhaps unknown, students via e-mail and the Internet, for example.

**New Tools for Storytelling**

Traditional schools assume that when children tell back what they have heard or memorized, they have mastered content. We all know that this may not be the case. But when children can tell what they have learned through stories - that is, demonstrating understanding in their own words and pictures based in personal experience - we can see what they know and don't know.

In today's classrooms, technology tools can provide many opportunities for children to communicate and extend their understanding of what they know and their place in the world. For example, the CyberFair contest, another Global SchoolNet program, provides a way for children to share unique information with others around the world. CyberFair is "an international challenge where students produce a Web site that tells a story about how people or programs in their own local communities use education to help make the world better, friendlier or safer." (As part of the contest, students review other contestants' Web sites against a rubric in which success at clear communication of purpose and content is reflected in the scoring.)

The idea of digital storytelling - telling stories and sharing information through multimedia - was inaccessible to most students and teachers until recently. Now, in this "digital age," computers, video cameras, editing software, graphics programs, and an array of such tools allow students and teachers to share what they are doing in many ways to a worldwide audience.

Joe Lambert, co-founder of the Center for Digital Storytelling, says, "The digital storytelling community has described the Internet and new media explosion as a release to a century of pent up frustration at being involved in a one way discourse; electronic media speaks at us but we could not talk back. We want to talk back, not on the terms of the governors of media empires, but on our own terms. We want the full diversity of expressions to be available, even if we ignore most of them, most of the time."

While Canadian storyteller, Dan Yashinsky, was not speaking of teachers or students in the quote below, I would like to apply his words to the importance of story in education. "To be a storyteller means knowing stories in your head," he says. "It means knowing how to say them out loud, getting the words right, making pictures with your words. And it especially means finding the 'next' teller," that is, another person who will take your story and add to it through his or her understanding and experience. In this way, students deepen their understanding of the people and events that they learn about in school, so that knowledge can be extended and new discoveries made. Telling a good story - about an event in history, in response to a book or a movie, even as evidence of how the particulars of a mathematician's life provided the context for his or her mathematical breakthrough - supports and enhances teaching and learning.

Since we all recognize that, as David Thornburg has often said, "We must prepare our students for their future, not our past," helping them tell the best stories in as many ways possible seems fundamental.

It all comes back to clear communication, which is a reflection of deep thought and an array of experiences. When students are encouraged to become master storytellers, they can prove what they know, and have gone a long way down the path towards contributing their own unique gifts to the human enterprise.

Celia Genishi and Anne Haas Dyson sum up the importance of stories: "Stories help us construct our selves, who used to be one way and are now another; stories help to make sense of, evaluate, and integrate the tensions inherent in experience: the past with the present, the fictional with the "real," the official with the unofficial, the personal with the professional, the canonical with the different or unexpected. ...Perhaps in the end, we need our stories to give us hope. They help us see possibilities, they give us what we need to envision a transformed future in which learners have satisfying social relationships, make sense of print, all see themselves in the world around them - in dolls they favor, the books they choose, and the stories they tell, hear, read, write, perform."

*Heard a good story lately? A good story will bring people together, share dreams, get a point across, even change the world!* --Jay Goldspinner

**References:**

Brody, Ed *et al.* (2002) *Spinning Tales, Weaving Hope: Stories, Storytelling and Activities for Peace, Justice and the Environment,* New Society Publishers, B.C., Canada.

Cousineau, Phil (2001) *Once and Future Myths: The Power of Ancient Stories in Modern Times,* Conari Press, CA.

Dyson, Anne Haas and Genishi, Celia, eds. (1994) *The Need for Story: Cultural Diversity in Classroom and Community,* National Council of Teachers of English, IL.

Lakoff, George, and Johnson, Mark (1980) *Metaphors We Live By,* University of Chicago Press, IL.

Lambert, Joe (2002) *Digital Storytelling: Capturing Lives, Creating Community,* Digital Diner Press, CA.

McDonald, Margaret Read (1992) *Peace Tales: World Folktales to Talk About,* Linnet Books, CT.

Rodari, Gianni (1973, 1996) *The Grammar of Fantasy: An Introduction to the Art of Inventing Stories,* Teachers and Writers Collaborative, NY.

Schank, Roger C (1990) *Tell Me A Story: A New Look at Real and Artificial Memory,* Charles Scribner's Sons, NY.

Silko, Leslie Marmon (1977) *Ceremony,* Penguin Books, NY.

Silko, Leslie Marmon (1981) *Storyteller,* Arcade Publishing, NY.

Yashinsky, Dan (1994) *Next Teller: A Book of Canadian Storytelling,* Ragweed Press, R.E.I., Canada.

Yolen, Jane (1992) *Storyteller,* The NESFA Press, MA.

Yolen, Jane (2000) *Touch Magic: Fantasy, Faerie & Folklore in the Literature of Childhood,* August House Publishers, Inc., AK.

# Extending the Information Revolution with Digital Equity and Inclusion

Bonnie Bracey
tcpd2020@aol.com

Today, interactive multimedia technology provides us with new ways to draw upon children's natural impulses. These new media offer an abundance of materials including text, voice, music, graphics, photos, animation and video. But they offer more than abundance. Bringing all of these media together in convergence means that we can vastly expand the range of learning experiences that open up the social and natural worlds to children. A major focus of efforts, funds, and other support must be directed to making sure all children have access to these technologies, and all their teachers are well versed in the value and use of technology tools.

When students can go beyond memorizing facts, they can begin to explore relationships among ideas and thus experience a more connected form of learning in which formerly separate school subjects are brought together into a clear context. Students then see direct "real world" applications for what they are learning in school.

Even more important, because these new media are interactive, they engage students in active, focused learning. Students can also choose various learning paths, and they have the media available to record, link, and extend what they learn. Even better, when students have traveled a particular learning path, they can go back and deepen their work depending on their interests and individual needs, as well as move forward to new levels for further exploration of ideas or continued learning.

But teachers must be recognized as the crucial link between the child and the technological environment, between the child and bodies of knowledge.

**What Is a Teacher?**

The typical definition of teacher in the dictionary (*e.g.,* "one who instructs") needs to be changed to fit today's world. No longer is the image of an adult in a classroom with 20-40 students in desks in rows accurate. In fact, in many countries, there are virtual teachers for students who are engaged in distance learning. In Australia and New Zealand, for example, distance learning has been in use for a long time. Radio is also a powerful tool for teachers in some places in the world. Now we have global links between classrooms via the Internet, and other ways of creating learning (and sharing ideas about teaching and learning) using technology.

There are also many powerful varieties of hands-on learning in indigenous societies. Sometimes what happens between teachers and learners may not even be recognized by the majority culture as school, but teachers and students in these situations are deeply engaged in the important transmission of culture, history and ideas.

In some countries, teachers work together in cooperative-teaching groups in which a teacher moves up with his or her class, and several teachers are involved with every class.

Nowhere in dictionary definitions of teacher will you find magician, missionary, time manager, social worker or deft manipulator of time. But all of these words - depending on the location of the school in which one is teaching - have become a part of the description of the occupation. As the world has gotten more complicated the job of teaching has also changed and gotten increasingly complex.

Fortunately, there are mentors, virtual (online) teachers, experts who assist teachers, and teachers, children and communities involved in project based learning, which can bring together the ancient ways of teaching and learning with the new ways of helping children turn information into knowledge with the aid of telecommunications and other multimedia tools.

As described on The George Lucas Educational Foundation's Web site (http://www.glef.org), in project-based learning, students work in teams to explore real-world problems and create presentations to share what they have learned. Compared with learning solely from textbooks, this approach has many benefits for students, including:

- Deeper knowledge of subject matter;
- Increased self-direction and motivation;
- Improved research and problem-solving skills.

## New Tools for New Times

The ideal learning environment would, as Peter Marin once said, "Satisfy children's curiosity by presenting them with new things to be curious about."

The environment should engage children in exploring, thinking, reading, writing, researching, inventing, problem solving, and experiencing the world. "Some schools and communities offer variable resources. The job of the teacher is to take the resources and materials available and fashion them into something that works, for that individual class, in that school, in that community in that part of the world," Marin explained.

The job of the teacher, then, is to work within the philosophy of the time and place, but not rule out inquiry and innovation. So, teaching for understanding should be based on many factors, and assessed in a variety of ways. Students can be held accountable for information on low stakes and high stakes tests and practices, be helped to reveal the depth of conceptual understanding they need in order to continue deepening their knowledge and to take them to the next level of work, and participate fully in exploring the most significant ideas underlying course content.

Hopefully, the basis for learning is what John Dewey (1943) identified nearly a century ago as the greatest educational resource - the child's natural impulses to inquire or to find out things; to use

24

language and thereby to enter into the social world; to build or make things; and to express [his] feelings and ideas. Dewey saw these impulses, rather than the traditional disciplines, as the foundation for the curriculum. The educational challenge for the teacher is to nurture these impulses for lifelong learning. And project-based learning as a practice lends itself to supporting each child's natural propensity for exploration and understanding.

Personally, I no longer stop at the teacher store looking for ideas and new ways of working with curriculum, books, hands-on materials, and ideas. Those visits have been replaced with resources - and connections to mentors and other teachers around the world - I find on the Internet. When I started, many of the resources were new to me and gave depth to my knowledge. I could explore subject matter areas, look at lesson plans if I desired, but more important than lesson plans was the ability to access learning places that were often open when school was open and closed by the time school ended. There were also places to buy things if I chose to. And a very special part of the online experience can be found in invitations to be involved in professional learning experiences - often without cost.

I found that students could interact with other children who were learning the same subjects, in many parts of the world. What intrigued me most was that with project-based learning activities reflecting the standards and objectives children needed to master, students at all levels were able to work in teams to explore real-world problems and create presentations to share what they have learned.

The large issue, of course, is access for teachers. While it may be the case that virtually all of the schools in this country contain at least one Internet connection, it is also true that many teachers still have not been given the support necessary to become true integrators of technology in their work. I am going to suggest two solutions - both of which will be more or less successful depending on the time and technology access available to teachers.

**Mentors and Models**

Mentoring is very important in any profession. In teaching in particular, because of the solitary nature of many classrooms, teachers can gain fresh perspectives on their work. Teacher mentors can be a peer, a former teacher, a parent, an expert in a field of interest, some other special person who provides guidance, a group on a listserv, or an organization. Teachers can participate in action research projects, online or off, that focus on particular classroom practices and extend the understanding of those involved.

My action research started with the National Education Association's (NEA) National Foundation for Improvement in Education (NFIE) project a number of years ago. While the program in which I participated is no longer taking place, resources are available that speak directly to mentoring possibilities at the NEA/NFIE Web site: http://www.nfie.org/publications/mentoring.htm.

Many professional education associations offer a variety of resources for mentoring. These groups are subgroups of what I call the ABC's of education. The National Council of Teachers of Mathematics (NCTM: http://www.nctm.org/), the National Science Teachers Association (NSTA: http://www.nsta.org/), the National Council for Geographic Education (NCGE: http://www.geog.okstate.edu/ncge/), National Council of the Social Studies (NCSS: http://www.ncss.org/) - these are membership groups of particular disciplines in teaching and learning, and there are many I did not mention. There are inherent benefits in being connected with the organization of a discipline in which you are particularly interested.

The benefits of being in groups like these include access to recognized leaders, a connection to the ideas of the group, opportunities for leadership within the organization (including mentoring others!), and the nurturing of possibilities for learning, growing, and developing friends in the group who will be drawn to you, or you to them.

The world continues to change. To be effective, teachers must have access to technology, and be encouraged and supported to learn to use new technological tools for the benefit of their students. Equal access at all levels is essential for teachers so that the growing diverse population of students can be well served. Given the slightest chance, teachers will regularly seek out the learning campfire and return, ready to light the interest in their students for lifelong paths of inquiry.

**Resources for the Journey:**

*A Selection of Social Studies Web Sites:*
The National Geographic Society
    http://www.nationalgeographic.com/education/
Map Machine
    http://plasma.nationalgeographic.com/mapmachine/
Silk Road Project
    http://www.silkroadproject.org/

Remote Sensing Task Force

http://www2.oneonta.edu/~baumanpr/ncge/rstf.htm

Xpeditions

http://www.nationalgeographic.com/xpeditions/

The Digital Classroom

http://www.archives.gov/digital_classroom/index.html

American Memory Project from the Library of Congress

http://memory.loc.gov/

The African American Mosaic Exhibition by the Library of Congress

http://lcweb.loc.gov/exhibits/african/afam001.html

Explore Your Family History at Ellis Island

http://www.ellisislandrecords.org/

Journey to Tikal

http://www.destination360.com/tikal/guide.htm

*A Selection of Science Web Sites*

Watch NASA TV Now!

http://www.nasa.gov/ntv/

Volcano World

http://volcano.und.nodak.edu/vw.html

Windows to the Universe

http://www.windows.ucar.edu/tour/link=/windows3.html

The Jason Project

http://www.jasonproject.org/

The Ocean Planet

http://seawifs.gsfc.nasa.gov/ocean_planet.html

NASA Teacher Workshops

http://education.nasa.gov/new/

Exploratorium

http://www.exploratorium.org

NCSA Education, Outreach, and Training

http://www.ncsa.uiuc.edu/Divisions/eot/

The NCSA Education, Outreach, and Training (EOT) Division develops and conducts a wide variety of activities and programs for educators, engineers, scientists, and other learners. These activities disseminate advanced technologies to new and established communities to encourage audiences to adopt new computational technologies as learning tools in K-12 schools, colleges, universities, and the workplace. EOT staff work with NCSA's Access and Inclusion program to increase the participation of women and underrepresented groups in computational science and engineering and to foster relationships with minority-serving institutions.

*A Selection of Teaching and Learning Sites*

The Inquiry Page

http://www.inquiry.uiuc.edu/index.php3

Based at the University of Illinois, Urbana-Champaign, according to its Web page, "The Inquiry Page is more than a website; it's a dynamic virtual community where inquiry-based education can be discussed, resources and experiences shared, and innovative approaches explored in a collaborative

29

environment. Here you can search a growing database of inquiry units, and you can also build your own inquiry units. You can see pictures of inquiry-based activities and learn more about some of our partners who use inquiry methods. Learn how to assess and evaluate inquiry-based education or look for more inquiry resources to support what you're doing.

The Concord Consortium

http://www.concord.org/

The Concord Consortium is a nonprofit educational research and development organization based in Concord, Massachusetts. They create interactive materials that exploit the power of information technologies. Their primary goal in all of their work is digital equity - improving learning opportunities for all students.

Center for Innovative Learning Technologies (CILT)

http://www.cilt.org/

According to their Web site, CILT is a "distributed center designed to serve as a national resource for stimulating research on innovative, technology-enabled solutions to critical problems in K-14 learning. Our approach is to foster and conduct collaborative research and development in areas that we believe promise significant advances in learning."

The George Lucas Educational Foundation (GLEF)

http://www.glef.org

At the GLEF Web site, users will find articles, short video segments, interviews, and instructional modules that highlight good teaching and learning in classrooms and districts across the country. Project-based learning, technology integration, emotional intelligence, and system wide change are a few of the topics addressed. All materials can be freely downloaded and used in education.

*Education Reform Portals*

http://www.edreform.net

This Web site provides access to a variety of resource collections, including technology applications in learning, data driven reform, preservice technology infusion, professional development, equity, technology planning, digital equity, urban teacher education, and PDS (professional development schools) partnerships. The site is part of the United States Department of Education Technology Innovation Challenge Grant program; the portal is produced by the National Institute for Community Innovations.

# Visual Literacy:
## What You Get Is What You See (WYGIWYS™)

Lynell Burmark, Ph.D.

tcpd2020@aol.com

*The material in this chapter is part of an upcoming book by the author titled, What You GET is What You See (WYGIWYS).*

Have you gone behind the scenes of a Web page lately? Or received an e-mail that looks like this:

```
<CENTER>
L<!W>ack<!R>  <!I>of<!U>  S<!X>ch<!M>ooling
H<!H>ol<!K>din<!I>g<!W>  <!I>B<!N>ac<!U>k  You<!X>r
<!C>C<!D>ar<!M>eer<!P>?
```

Did you know that in the early days of word processing (circa 1980) you had to use these kinds of markings to indicate where you wanted to insert a graphic or write anything besides plain text? Commands had to be placed before and after the image, or any text you wanted in boldface, italics, larger size, or centered, etc. And unlike today's user-friendly Web authoring tools that let you switch back and forth between the HTML coded editing and the final picture views, with the early word processors you had to print out the page to see what you were creating was going to look like. This was not a domain for anyone short on patience... or paper!

Then came a major breakthrough in word processing software where what you could see on the screen represented what you would get when you printed it out. To celebrate this momentous achievement, the term What You See Is What You Get (WYSIWYG) was coined and the acronym (pronounced whizzywig) made it into the daily parlance of delighted computer users.

**From WYSIWYG to WYGIWYS™**

When my Thornburg Center colleague Lou Fournier was reviewing my book, *Visual Literacy: Learn to See, See to Learn* (Burmark, 2002), with his amazing ability to condense 100 pages into one sentence, he said: "So, what you're talking about is WYGIWYS?"

"Wiggywhiz?" I inquired, cluelessly.

"Yes," chimed Lou. "What You Get Is What You See. WYGIWYS™. You can't understand or 'get' anything until you have a mental image to hook it on."

Getting more and more excited, I replied: "This has serious implications for education. If teachers want all their students 'on the same page,' they really have to introduce their lessons – especially new concepts – with images before bombarding the students with words."

"Precisely," opined the big picture synthesizer. "Remember, you wrote a book to help teachers do just that!"

## From Books to Live Presentations

It's one thing to write a book (in the privacy of your own home office). It's another to put it into practice (in front of hundreds of people in a conference hotel ballroom). I had no trouble putting together the outrageous outfit you see here:

Hot pink hair, big turquoise sunglasses. It's the real me. ;-) Knowing that we are all quick to judge from appearances, I thought I could come into a session dressed like this and then see how seriously the audience took me and my presentation.

Although friends and colleagues have dared — okay, double-dared — me to make a pink-haired entrance for real, I haven't had the nerve to do so . . . as yet. What I did do was send a slide to teacher friends at the middle school and high school level to get students' reactions to the image. Without identifying me, my friends asked their students to write down what they thought of the pink lady: age, occupation, character, thoughts, etc.

Trevor, a middle schooler, wrote: This lady is 45 years old. She is an undercover FBI agent. She is a nice person but could be different in her disguises. She is probably thinking about how she can see who is going to steal the Mona Lisa painting.

Liz, a high schooler, wrote: This woman grew up in a middle to upper class society because she has straight teeth, meaning when she was younger she had braces. Her real age is of no importance. She is young at heart; you can tell by the smile. Material possessions aren't of any value because she isn't wearing any jewelry. That and she probably spends a lot of time around children who like to pull on necklaces and earrings. She has light brown hair that she doesn't feel she needs to dye, despite incoming gray hairs. She is comfortable with who she is.

What were the students doing in these cases? How much of their judgment came from associating my photo with images of comparable people in their lives or whom they had seen in movies or on television? Particularly in Liz's case, how much did her life experience and her own "issues" color her evaluation? Do you think she had braces? Wanted braces? Had a mother who wore expensive jewelry? Dyed her hair?

## The Power of First Impressions

We spend our lives filling the hard drive of our minds with images and we do our best to file new information where it best connects to or associates with data that is already there. Pink hair? More apt to be a nightclub singer than a college professor. Five nose rings and several visible tattoos? More apt to be a biker than an Episcopal priest. Is this prejudice or just the mind trying to make sense of a universe bombarding it with images?

And it isn't just people we judge by first impressions. The strongest and most indelible impressions of places come from their initial, visual impact. As feng shui expert William Spear writes: "First impressions account for more than 50% of the entire experience of a place. We create impressions in the early stages of experiencing an environment, and they remain a nearly indelible part of it even as changes occur and we process new information." (Spear, 1995.)

## Where the Eye Goes

Where does the eye go in this yin yang rendering of boring text (computer generated ones and zeroes) and playful images? As the Adobe ad proclaims, we are drawn to images (and, therefore, should use Photoshop and PageMaker to edit and place those images into attractive documents!).

## Color Power

Of course, in the Adobe ad and in my slide shows, the image is in color and the color draws the eye as much if not more than the images themselves.

As research by 3M Corporation was reported in the article, "The Power of Color in Presentations" (3M, 2001a):

- Color visuals increase willingness to read by up to 80%.
- Using color can increase motivation and participation by up to 80%.
- Color enhances learning and improves retention by more than 75%.

Approximately 80% of our impression of a product is based on its color. (Kinko's, 2000.) Advertisers understand this and use color in wrapping their goods so they appear to meet our needs. They know that our autonomic response to the colors, rather than the aesthetics of the packaging, determines what we buy. (Wagner, 1985.)

What are the implications of this for educators? Traditionally, we think of color as the decorative element for our bulletin boards:

orange for Halloween, Thanksgiving and the autumn leaves; pastels for Easter and spring; and so on. But color is much more than decoration. We are biologically programmed to respond to the colors we see:

| | |
|---|---|
| Red | Danger, excitement |
| Blue | Calm, security |
| Pink | Tranquility, relaxation |
| Green | Fertility, creativity |

And other colors evoke predictable responses:

Yellow is the most attention grabbing of all the 16.7 million colors the human eye can see. (Think of yellow highlighters. Why do they work so well?)

Black signals authority and finality. (Think of judges' robes and the "fade to black" screens for scene changes in movies. Consider judicious use of black in your own slideshow presentations.)

Researchers at Loyola College have documented the impact of color on comprehension and recall. (Hoadley, *et al.*, 1995.) How could this knowledge be applied to preparing documents for classroom use?

| Activity | Improved Up To |
|---|---|
| Time to sort documents | 15% |
| Time to locate a target word within a document | 74% |
| Accuracy of comprehension | 77% |

What might be "target words" in your documents? Due dates? Key pieces of information? What color might you choose for those target words? Why have red pens been the preferred weapons of English teachers for decades?

As Carlton Wagner, color guru and author of Color Power expounds:

> Particularly yellow-based reds (tomato) are great attention-getters.
>
> They have the power to get noticed, quickly. There was an early belief that red (rather than yellow) was really the fastest color seen, and this early myth was the basis for red being used for fire engines and other emergency equipment. Red used in combination with yellow will get even more attention than either color alone. (Wagner, p110, 1985.)

For more information about color and suggestions for its use in classroom activities, please see Chapter 4 ("Color Power") in the author's book, Visual Literacy, (Burmark, 2002).

**Visual Processors**

We've all heard expressions like:

> Seeing is believing.
>
> I see what you mean.
>
> See, I told you so....

Robert L. Lindstrom, author of The BusinessWeek Guide to Multimedia Presentations, explains the physiological basis of this kind of "visual thinking":

> Of all our sense receptors, the eyes are the most powerful information conduit to the brain. They send information to the cerebral cortex through two optic nerves, each consisting of 1,000,000,000 nerve fibers. By comparison, each auditory nerve consists of a mere 30,000 fibers.
>
> Nerve cells devoted to visual processing . . . account for about 30% of the brain's cortex, compared to 8% for touch and 3% for hearing.
>
> With all the bandwidth to the brain, it's no wonder we perceive the world and communicate in visual terms. We read five times as fast as the average person talks. We register a full-color image, the equivalent of a megabyte of data, in a fraction of a second. (Lindstrom, 1999.)

According to 3M Corporation's research, humans process graphics 60,000 times faster than text. (3M, 2001b.) (This is possible because the visual/perceptual channel in the brain manipulates image elements simultaneously, while the linguistic/cognitive channel functions in a linear, sequential manner. (Pavio, 1986.))

I do a little experiment in my workshops to illustrate this difference between words and images. I start with a screen full of text and ask the audience to imagine the rose it describes:

> Imagine a single, beautiful pink rose in a lush bed of dark green leaves. It has just rained and there are drops of moisture on the rose and the leaves. The rose is in full bloom, with its petals opened out to the morning sun. The pink hue of the petals varies from a soft blush to a deep rose that is almost red. Such a beautiful blossom ... I can almost smell its perfume.

Then I move on to the next slide and ask how many people saw exactly my rose – the one I was so eloquently describing:

Why or why not? Which is more concrete – the image or the words? If you want everyone "on the same page," seeing the same flower at the same time, what is the fastest, most certain way to get them there (short of actually handing them the real rose)?

## Multimedia, Multiple Image Streams

Is it possible to overdo the use of images? Could too much multimedia actually be distracting? It's turning out that just the opposite is true.

Last August, at an extraordinary weeklong IBI Global (IBI, 2002) workshop in Los Angeles, California, I had the privilege of experiencing a breakthrough technology called Super Teaching. As we entered the hotel ballroom classroom for each segment of instruction, we received a multisensory welcome consisting of audio surround sound and three large screens displaying a variety of images to set the stage for what we were about to experience. From public domain footage of NASA space shuttles to breathtaking views of nature, our spirits were lifted, our eyes alerted, and our beta brain waves aroused for hyper-efficient learning. Although there were some 200 participants in the class, we bonded like a family because of many interactive activities and because some very talented – and sneaky – camera persons circulated through our ranks and captured our moments of joy and humor for the rest of the group to see. Rounds of cheers and applause encouraged our newfound friends as they appeared on the screens, demonstrating their mastery of course material.

One afternoon, after enjoying the multimedia stimulation for several days, we had a session where former Byron Center, Michigan, school superintendent Dr. William Skilling explained the technology and his technology teacher, Nick Sheltrown, gave a demonstration lesson on the Russian Revolution. In the space of ten minutes, Nick combined video footage, still images, text, and interactive questions into a lesson that simulated the experience of being the Tsar at that moment in history. With electronic feedback devices, we got to "vote" on which advisor to heed, and which uprising to quell, and then compare our choices to the ones that the Tsar actually made. Needless to say, I now have a much better understanding of why the royal family was executed than I did by reading a chapter about the revolution from my textbook in high school.

I was surprised by how much information we covered in such a short time and how people from all walks of life were all engaged in the learning. And what I thought would have been a distracting bombardment of multiple streams of visual media actually served to create greater focus and recall than normally experienced in the more passive, linear approach of traditional chalk-and-talk classrooms.

Nick also talked about the evolution of television programs over the past fifty years and what that means in terms of how the current generation processes information. He invited us to contrast the simple plots in 1950s sitcoms like Leave It to Beaver with any of today's programs (or MTV videos) where dozens of characters weave in and out with subplots too numerous to mention (let alone follow!).

In watching coverage of the war in Iraq, I could not help but notice this same kind of evolution in television news. Between the retired generals with their multimedia maps, the politicians and public relations commentators from Washington, D.C., the dozens of embedded journalists reporting from battlefronts in Iraq and Kuwait, "experts" from all over the globe, interviews with soldiers' family members back in the States, and the occasional sound byte from President Bush himself, we were omnipresent for all the action related to the war. And even when the anchor person was sitting behind a desk – just to make sure we didn't miss any late-breaking news – there was a constant march of text across the bottom of the screen. (Imagine CBS having done that to Walter Cronkite!)

How do we respond to this kind of barrage? Are we able to absorb and retain that much information at once? In an article posted on the Super Teaching web site (Pulos, 2002), Dr. Lee Pulos explains that learning is actually enhanced by this kind of environment. He shares the response of one student to a powerful multimedia lesson, "It was the difference of driving down the highway at 30 M.P.H. and experiencing meandering distractions versus driving at 80 M.P.H. and taking in everything because you are so focused." Pulos also cites the experiment conducted by Festinger and Macoby to determine if a group of students engaged in two tasks simultaneously would be distracted sufficiently to lower their score on an assignment. One group listened to a taped lecture while watching a highly entertaining silent movie. The control group just listened to the tape. The subjects who were distracted by the film actually "learned and returned information more easily and displayed more mental flexibility than those who were not distracted!" (Festinger and Macoby, 1964.)

**Focus on Learning . . . the Natural Way**

The Super Teaching folks recommend another practice that I have been advocating for years: project images of the majesty of Nature and play classical music as students come into the classroom. This helps them leave their more harried world with all its baggage at the door and entrain their brain waves to the optimal rhythms for learning.

[NOTE: See Chapter 8 ("Good Vibrations") of the book *Enlighten Up! An Educator's Guide to Stress-Free Living* (Fournier and Burmark, 2003) where my co-author Lou Fournier expounds on purposeful use of music in the classroom.]

## Bringing Images into the Classroom

Convinced that using more images could enhance teaching and accelerate learning in your classroom? So, where do you get the images? There are three broad categories of resources:

1. Scanning student work

There are several advantages to using student drawings. First, they give you access to the child's imagination and a window into their perspective on the world. As Elliot Eisner, professor of education and art at the Stanford University School of Education, has pointed out:

> Children leave their own personal 'thumbprint' on each of the images they create. Objects that matter to them the most take on a visual significance in their work. Children tend to exaggerate those aspects of a drawing, painting, or sculpture that are most meaningful to them. (Eisner and Trela-Berger, 1996.)

2. Using digital cameras

With high-resolution digital cameras the size of a deck of cards costing less than $300 each, there is no excuse not to put cameras into the hands of students. Let them be the eyes and ears and bring their perspective of the world into the classroom.

3.     Downloading images from the Web

Try using a search engine like Google.com and type in the word "images." The last time I did that I got 13.9 million hits. Or use the image search function of Google or any of the other search engines (e.g., Lycos Image Gallery, Yahoo! Picture Gallery, Altavista Photo and Media Finder). They quickly generate hundreds or even thousands of pictures of the specific item(s) you'd like to see illustrated.

Some excellent sites for useful images include:

| | |
|---|---|
| Pics 4 Learning | **<http://pics.tech4learning.com/pics>** |
| Astronomy Pic of the Day | **<http://antwrp.gsfc.nasa.gov/apod>/** |
| Web Museum | **<http://metalab.unc.edu/wm/paint>** |
| Civil War | **<http://memory.loc.gob/ammem/cwpht ml/cwphome.html>** |
| Holocaust | **<www.remember.org>** |
| Images of 20th Century | **<www.nara.gov>** |
| Great Images in NASA | **<http://grin.hq.nasa.gov>** |

**"I didn't think ... until I saw...."**

A letter from a little boy to God was recently circulating on the Web:

> *Dear God,*
>
> *I didn't think orange went with purple*
> *until I saw the sunset you made on Tuesday.*
> *That was cool.*
>
> > *– Eugene*

It was only when he had seen the glorious orange and purple sunset that Eugene could conceive of that color combination. First the vision, then the cognition. The very word idea comes from the Greek idein, meaning to see. (Armstrong, 2003.)

Of course this all plays out at a subconscious level. But let's bring it home with a little activity you can try in your classroom. (Meltzer)

Ask your students to take out a piece of 8.5 x 11" paper and fold it in half horizontally to create two 5.5" high by 8.5" wide sections. On the top half, have them draw a cat.

On the bottom half have them draw a meerkat.

If they've seen the movie, The Lion King, that will not be a problem. If they have not seen the movie, been to a zoo, or visited the deserts and plains of the Kalahari Desert in Bostwana lately, drawing a meerkat could be a real challenge.

To make the point about drawing from experience (literally), you might ask students to sketch the meerkat and then show them the story of a meerkat family in the Alain Degré documentary, Return to Meerkat Valley, which was aired on the Discovery Channel. Then ask them again to draw a meerkat, complete with its habitat and some of its favorite foods. Was it easier to draw the animal after seeing the documentary? Why? What if the teacher read a story about the meerkats without showing any illustrations?

**"Text is toast."**

This proclamation from futurist Geoffrey Meredith (Meridith, 1999) argues that too heavy reliance on visual imagery will be the death of text. While there is plenty of evidence to support his argument –

- 22% of college students would rather pick up trash than write a paper;
- 47% would rather donate blood! (Newsweek, 2001.)

– teachers are consistently finding that when students start with an image their vocabulary is richer and their writing is more colorful.

Remember in elementary school when we would draw something on the top two-thirds of the page and then write a few sentences below? Did anyone ever have trouble coming up with those few sentences? Remember in high school when we were challenged to fill a blank sheet of paper (or nowadays a blank computer screen)? Did anyone ever experience writers' block?

A wonderful federally-funded project called "Image Making in the Writing Process" invited first-graders to create collages from an assortment of colored tissue papers. The language the students expressed to describe their collages (e.g., "clouds like fluffy pink pancakes") was richer and literally more colorful than what they would have generated without the visual inspiration. (Olshansky, 1994.)

Why did the vocabulary of the average 14 year old drop from 25,000 to 10,000 words between 1950 and 1999? (Time, 2000.) My theory is that decline is due, at least in part, to the practice of taking the crayons away by the time kids reach third grade. Let me draw the story from the right side of my brain and the left side will gleefully find the words to describe that story!

## Dual Coding

Yes, visual and verbal information are encoded and decoded by separate, specialized perceptual and cognitive channels in the brain. (This is what Allan Pavio calls "dual coding.") But, as Pavio explains, the brain involves these independent systems so concepts can flow seamlessly between their linguistic labels and their visual representations. (Pavio, 1986.)

My colleague and friend, Thomas Armstrong, has a chapter called "Seeing the Visual Basis of Literacy" in his latest book, *The Multiple Intelligences of Reading and Writing* (Armstrong, 2003). He talks about the visual aspect of letters themselves and about visualizing the words we read.

If there was ever any doubt:

And think about how different typefaces evoke different emotions on a subconscious level:

*Wedding Invitation*
IRS tax return
𝕾𝖍𝖆𝖐𝖊𝖘𝖕𝖊𝖆𝖗𝖊

Could you use the Aristocrat, Helvetica, and Old English typefaces interchangeably? Not unless you were seeking a humorous or shocking impact!

And when we read a word, at the same time as we decipher it phonetically, we are searching our stored memories for a visual clue as to its meaning. Take the word tree, for instance. Ask a student in Tacoma, Washington, Olean, New York, and West Palm Beach, Florida to draw a tree. Odds are high that you would get an evergreen fir, a sugar maple, and a palm tree. Same four-letter word. Different life experiences.

As we saw with the example of the pink rose, we bring our (visual) life experiences to the words we hear and read.

**Both Sides Now**

In "Teaching Visual Literacy in a Multimedia Age," Glenda Rakes explains that by combining visuals and text we can increase comprehension.

> Using positron emission tomography (PET scans), medical researchers have been able to demonstrate that different areas of the brain become active when individuals are exposed to verbal and visual information. When individuals were asked to look at and remember verbal information, two regions in the brain's verbal domain – the left hemisphere – became active. When presented with visual information, the right hemisphere lit up.

> Given this information, the use of visuals in instructional materials takes on a larger dimension than when simply thought of as decorative supplements to text. The use of visuals with text can provide that dual code that can, in turn, increase comprehension. (Rakes, 1999)

Award-winning teacher, Jerome Burg, has put this theory into exquisite practice in his high school English classroom. He assigns groups of students to read classic works of literature and then demonstrate their understanding by creating short comic book versions of the works. Can you guess what play the following frame was depicting?

What about the second language classroom? Why not have some fun with proverbs in the target language? Try dividing the class into 4-5 groups of students. Assign each group a proverb to illustrate, then ask them to pass their drawing on to the next group to translate into words. A few examples (for a Spanish or English as a Second Language classroom) might include:

| | |
|---|---|
| El amor es ciego. | Love is blind. |
| No todo lo que brilla es oro. | All that glitters is not gold. |
| Donde hay humo, hay calor. | Where there's smoke, there's fire. |
| En boca cerrada no entran moscas. | A closed mouth catches no flies. |
| Más puede la pluma que la espada. | The pen is mightier than the sword. |
| Más vale pájaro en mano que cien volando. | Better a bird in the hand than 100 flying (than two in the bush). |

In a 1982 study, Levie and Lentz reported findings from 55 experiments comparing learning from illustrated text versus text alone. They noted that illustrations contributed to reader interest and enjoyment, affected attitudes and emotions, and provided spatial information that was difficult to express in words. They also calculated that groups using illustrated texts performed 36% better than groups using text alone on measured criteria. (Levie and Lentz, 1982.)

***

In the end, it's not either/or, but the synergistic juxtaposition of both words and images that we want to use in instruction. Our students must learn to process both words and pictures. They must be able to move gracefully and fluently between text and images, between literal and figurative worlds.

## References

3M Corporation research (2001a) 3M Meeting Network Articles & Advice (2001) [Online article]. Available: <www.3m.com/meetingnetwork/readingroom/meetingguide_power_color.html>

3M Corporation research (2001b) 3M Meeeting Network Articles & Advice (2001) [Online article]. Available: <www.3m.com/meetingnetwork/readingroom/meetingguide_pres.html>

Armstrong, Thomas (2003) *The Multiple Intelligences of Reading and Writing*, Association for Supervision and Curriculum Development.

Burmark, Lynell (2002) *Visual Literacy: Learn to See, See to Learn,* Association for Supervision and Curriculum Development (ASCD), Alexandria, VA.

Eisner, Elliot, and Trela-Berger, Anne (1996) "Looking at Art Through the Mind's Eye," **Stanford Educator,** Stanford University School of Education News, Spring 1996, pages 2, 12.

Festinger, L. & Macoby, J. (1964) "On resistance to persuasive communications," **Journal of Abnormal & Social Psychology,** 1964, v. 68, pages 359-366.

Fournier, Lou and Burmark, Lynell (2003) *Enlighten Up! An Educator's Guide to Stress-Free Living,* Association for Supervision and Curriculum Development (ASCD), Alexandria, VA.,

Hoadley, Ellen, *et al.* (1995) "Investigating the Effects of Color, Fonts, and Bold Text in Documents," Working Paper #WP0196.029, David D. Lattanze Center for Executive Studies in Information Systems, Loyola College, Baltimore, MD, 1995. [Online article.] Available: <http://lattanze.loyola.edu/frames/research/wp0196.029.html>

IBI (2002) IBI Global operates one of the most sophisticated management training programs in the world. Five, week long residency programs are offered annually. Real time business mission execution is conducted all week as core teams reinvent cooperative business systems. More information is available on the Web site: <www.ibi.org>

Kinkos, (2000) "Brand Packaging magazine noted recently that 80% of a consumer's buying decision is based on color." Quoted in **Kinko's Impress** (Issue 1/2000), page 15.

Levie, W. H. and Lentz, R. (1982) "Effects of Text Illustrations: A Review of Research," **Educational Communication and Technology Journal, 30** (4), pages 195-232.

Lindstrom, Robert L. (1999) "Being Visual: The Emerging Visual Enterprise," **Business Week,** *Special Advertising Section,* April 19, 1999.

Meltzer, Bonnie (undated) The idea of drawing a series of animals (from the familiar to the not familiar) came from Portland, Oregon art educator Bonnie Meltzer.

Meredith, Geoffrey (1999) "The Demise of Writing," **The Futurist,** Bethesda, Maryland, October 1999, pages 27-30.

Newsweek (2001) "Periscope," **Newsweek,** April 2, 2001, page 9.

Olshansky, Beverly (1994) "Making Writing a Work of Art: Image-making within the Writing Process," **Language Arts,** September 1994, 71(5), pages 350-56.

Pavio, Allan (1986) *Mental Representations: A dual coding approach,* Oxford University Press, New York.

Pulos, Lee (2002) *Super Teaching to Quantum Learning,* document located at <www.stconcepts.com>

Rakes, Glenda C. (1999) "Teaching Visual Literacy in a Multimedia Age," **TechTrends,** Washington D.C., September 1999.

Spear, William (1995) *Feng Shui Made Easy,* San Francisco: Harper Collins Publishers, page 63.

TIME (2000) "Numbers," **TIME,** February 14, 2000, page 25.

Wagner, Carlton (1985) *Color Power,* Chicago, Wagner Institute for Color Research,, pages 37-38.

# *Purposeful Use of Music*

Lou Fournier

louphonia@earthlink.net

*Music is love in search of a word.*
*– Ambrose Bierce*

The universe is one vast orchestra. We are its instruments.

What we hear, what we sing, what we play are expressions of the resonance we experience, as creatures of nature, from nature all around us. And while this description might seem merely rhapsodic, it turns out to be almost literally true. Rodgers and Hammerstein didn't have it quite right: Far more than just the hills are alive with the sound of music.

I've always found it telling that you can make music with a blade of grass. As with choosing any good instrument, you need to pick the blade carefully: you want a nice, smooth, thick one. You carefully position the blade of grass vertically between your thumbs. You blow over the grass in the little space that forms just below your knuckles. It's a crude reed instrument; you can't get much tonal variation, of course. But you can get quite a musical sound as your breath causes the grass to vibrate.

Doing this as a kid, I considered that there must be a very close connection between music and nature. In recent years, research on sound and its properties has come into its heyday, and that research shows more and more how much of a natural phenomenon music really is. And in the ultimate demonstration of making music with a natural object, there is an elderly man in Mexico who regularly makes news and draws sizable crowds as he performs very musically sophisticated concerts – on a leaf!

The fact is that everything in nature can be said to make a potential sound, because everything in nature vibrates. Much of natural vibration remains inaudible; we can hear sound only when vibrations occur in something capable of carrying sound waves to our ears, such as air or water. The quintessential sounds of nature that we do hear -- such as wind rustling through trees, the syncopation of bubbling water – are quintessentially musical.


When Pythagoras stated that the universe was filled with Music of the Spheres, he was saying that creation is inherently and thoroughly musical. From this perspective, music is not an invention of man; songs and symphonies are, but they are man's expressions of what he hears all around. Some musicologists say that music is organized sound, and by that definition the sounds occurring in nature are not, strictly speaking, music. But let us consider the quite reasonable possibility that nature has its own innate and remarkable sense of musical expression. There are times when nature does its own organizing of sound, with far more musically evocative results than our human efforts. Music as we typically understand it is, I believe, the human interpretation of the voice of nature.

Scientists discover more every day about the sounds made by the spheres whirling through the heavens. At the time of this writing there is a remarkable Web site at Stanford University where you can download files of the sounds the sun makes (http://solar-center.stanford.edu/singing/singing.html). Are these sounds music? Some would say no. But the poet within even the staid scientists of Stanford can't resist calling the site the Singing Sun.

But why does any of this matter? What difference does it make whether or not music arises from and is a deeply indigenous aspect of nature? I believe that understanding the "naturalness" of music enables us to use it in a much more focused and powerful way.

Use music? Don't we just listen to music?

No. No matter how seemingly undirected our thoughts are when we even casually play music at any time, we always have an intention behind it. We choose the music we listen to, even if ostensibly just for background and notwithstanding how seemingly innocuous such a choice seems. We don't always consciously know what that purpose is. And that's my point. Music can be used consciously and very purposefully, even if our desire is to effect an unconscious reaction such as relaxation. This purposefulness must consider two principle aspects of music. First, it must take into account the physical properties of sound itself on the human nervous system, a field of study called psychoacoustics. Second, it must consider the intent of the performer and composer or songwriter, for music is also a carrier of intentionality. If we don't make our musical choices consciously and with an appreciation of music's true power and influences, at best we won't take full advantage of it. At worst, we defeat our own best desires, sometimes with quite harmful consequences. And nowhere is this truer than in the classroom, where the purposeful use of music becomes an issue not only of educational enhancement - very important and powerful in and of itself - but also of serious responsibility.

## Good Vibrations

Music is known to have properties that enhance learning and alter moods. The "mind-alert/body-relaxed" use of music, pioneered by Bulgarian psychiatrist Georgi Lozanov, uses rhythm to slow down bodily functions and induce slower brain wave activity, both of which expand the brain's learning capacities. Indeed, music has long been used by casual listeners and health-care professionals alike to calm nerves and experience the pleasure of sound. But just as there is the beauty of a favorite soft and gentle melody, there is also the screeching of fingernails on the blackboard or the thundering of a jackhammer on the pavement just feet from your ears. The fact is that sound can be either greatly empowering or highly toxic depending on how it's used.

## Psychoacoustics

French physician and psychologist Alfred Tomatis, called by some the "Einstein of the ear," was an early pioneer in the development of psychoacoustics. Working through much of the latter half of the 20th century, Tomatis discovered that sound - in particular, certain frequencies of sound -- is actually a neurological nutrient that charges the neocortex of the brain. With these frequencies, our higher-order thinking skills become greatly enhanced; conversely, Tomatis discovered, other kinds of sounds can damage or discharge energy from the body.

What distinguishes healthful sounds from unhealthful ones? One of the most critical considerations is the frequency at which the sound vibrates. The normal range of hearing for humans is generally between 20 and 20,000 hertz, although some people can hear above 20,000 hertz, as can many animals, including dogs, dolphins, alligators, and elephants.

Everything physical - from people to the earth itself - has a frequency at which it most naturally vibrates. This is its resonant frequency. When we hear sounds that do not (literally) resonate with us, we get a sense of vague discomfort on one extreme to outright illness on the other. So what are the sounds that our brains thrive on? What exactly are those vibrations? According to the research of Tomatis, they are the higher frequencies of sound: Eighty percent of the neuroreceptors for sound respond only to frequencies above 3,000 hertz, and one-third of the charge that the ear supplies to the brain comes from these frequencies. Tomatis discovered that frequencies above 8,000 hertz provide enormous neurological benefit to the brain. To put this into some perspective, consider that typical human conversation ranges between 750 and 3,000 hertz. Optimal frequencies for charging the neocortex, then, are well above what we hear in our usual working day.

Ranges of human hearing influence different areas of our lives. Low frequencies - from 125 to 750 hertz - greatly influence the vestibular system and, therefore, have the greatest impact on the body. Human languages usually occur at midrange frequencies - 750 to 4,000 hertz - although some use frequencies up to 12,000 hertz.

Unfortunately, we live in a world that is largely unaware of the power of sound. Have you heard cars rolling down the street with the bass turned up loud enough to stun small animals a hundred yards away? Joshua Leeds, one of the most knowledgeable and dynamic presenters on the topic of psychoacoustics, calls such bass-heavy music "sonic Valium." This is because extended exposure to loud bass sounds tends to discharge cerebral energy, thereby dulling the physical senses. Joshua's concern for what he calls secondhand sound has led him to the forefront of a new movement he calls "sonic activism."

When I consult with schools about their music use, one of the first things I do is to check music playback systems everywhere in the building. The bass is almost always far heavier than it should be. Keeping the bass in proper balance is critically important to prevent physical burnout, especially for teachers who have music playing most of the school day (and perhaps continue to listen to it on their own time). Likewise, it's important to keep the upper frequencies turned up as high as the playback system will allow while still keeping the music pleasant. Reaching this balance often requires outside ears, because most people's sense of sonic balance itself is out of optimal balance; few people realize how toxic their listening habits have become.

Because I'm a musician as well as an educational consultant, I'm constantly asked by teachers, "What music should we play in the classroom?" This question is often posed with trepidation. Many educators fear a tense showdown with students (or even with each other) over issues of personal musical taste or cultural preference. The answer gracefully skirts all such issues, because it has to do almost entirely with psychoacoustics.

Any music that provides optimal neurological nutrients is acceptable in the classroom. Ideally, that means music recorded, mixed, and mastered with a high percentage of high acoustic frequencies and played with the best frequency balance possible. Interestingly, music tends to self-organize by broad categories when considered from a psychoacoustics perspective; for example, classical music is generally more healthful sonically than are many forms of contemporary popular music.

Even governmental agencies have come to realize the significance of psychoacoustics and have used their properties to remarkable benefit. The city of Vallejo, California, attracted international attention in the winter of 2001 when it started playing certain kinds of music over speakers in high petty-crime districts. The crime rate in these areas plummeted dramatically - "some 25 to 40 percent at the bus transfer station," according to Mark Mazzaferro, public information officer for the city. "We saw similar programs used successfully in New York, Montreal, and Boston, so we decided to give it a try here. At the bus station, the only thing that changed was the music." The program cost all of about $200 per site. "We just went down to Target and bought a CD player, speakers, and CDs," Mazzaferro says. "It was enough to do the job." People whose ears are psychoacoustically accustomed to particular musical properties have a very hard time tolerating sound that does not match those properties.

Listening habits can of course be changed, and there are numerous programs designed to do just that. Such programs can recondition the ears, first to discern the higher, healthier frequencies, and then to listen to them enjoyably. Some of these programs have demonstrated astonishing benefits for people suffering from a huge range of difficulties, from severe depression to autism.

## The Undercurrent of Overtones

Pythagoras is remembered today primarily for his famed geometry theorem, but musicians consider his most profound contribution to our knowledge to be his discovery of the overtone series. There is probably nothing that more powerfully demonstrates the astonishing, natural order of music - and it is further telling that overtones, being very high frequency sounds, are extremely important for the optimal charging of the neocortex.

Overtones, or harmonics, occur in all sounds made acoustically (that is to say, on non-electronic acoustic instruments such as guitars and pianos and by the human voice). Whenever we hear a note played on an instrument or sung by a voice, the note we hear seems to be a single sound. But in fact it's actually made up of many different tones all resonating simultaneously but in differing degrees of strength or prominence. The lowest tone of these frequencies is always the strongest and is the primary tone of the note we hear. The higher frequencies are those heard over the original tone - hence, the overtones. All the frequencies in the tone together help make up its "color" or natural tone, and it would sound very different and unmusical - unnatural - the overtones were not there.

Sound is carried on waves and is measured in vibrational cycles per second. The specific number of cycles per second determines the pitch of a particular tone. When you hear of an instrument being tuned to the standard pitch of A 440, for example, that means that it's being tuned to the note A, vibrating at a rate of 440 cycles per second.

Pythagoras took a single piece of string and stretched it across a board; he called this primitive "instrument" a monochord. With this simple device, he made an astonishing discovery of the correlation of music and its overtones with mathematics and, ultimately, with the nature of the universe itself. He found that if you divided the string into two equal portions, the sound made at that midpoint vibrated at a rate exactly twice that of the entire string. If the note of the whole string were the A 440 in our example above, for instance, when the string was divided in half, it then vibrated at a rate of 880 cycles per second. And the tone made at that midpoint was exactly an octave higher than the tone of the whole string. Likewise, when he divided the string into three equal portions, the tones produced at those points vibrated at a rate exactly three times that of the entire string. And so on: divided into four portions, the tones were exactly four times that of the entire string, and on indefinitely. There is an exact and absolutely predictable correlation, Pythagoras discovered, between equally divided lengths of a string and the vibrational rates of the tones produced at those intervals.

The mathematical precision of overtones seems amazing in itself, but the amazement mounts when we realize that the notes produced by the first several overtones produce a sound that is immensely pleasing - because they just happen to form a major chord! They include the tonic note (the fundamental and its octave notes), a perfect fifth, and a major third; these are the exact intervals of a standard major chord in Western tonality. The Western ear generally hears the early overtone notes more clearly than the later ones; it tends to most readily hear that major chord in the first handful of overtones. I believe this tendency helps explain our cultural predilection for music based on this tonality. We love simple music based around this sound. In other cultures, the ear hears and often favors the later overtones, which become increasingly microtonal; this may likewise help reveal why some cultures love to sing notes that Western tonal consciousness can barely recognize. Interestingly, though, even cultures deeply steeped in microtonality generally love the sound of "simple" Western music; Indian and Chinese audiences buy Western popular music by the truckloads.

It was a reasonable conclusion to Pythagoras that the overtone series and its mathematical precision were more than just coincidence. To him and many since, the overtone series was proof of a divine order in the universe. He considered the universe itself to be one vast monochord with one end of a cosmic string attached to the world of spirit and the other end connected to the world of matter. He believed that the study of music and the science of its intervals could bring one to a full understanding of creation. He wrote of the arrangement of the planets as notes on a musical scale, and he spoke of the Music of the Spheres. An entire school of mysticism formed around these beliefs, and it continues to this day. Small wonder, given that overtones, with their exact mathematical order and "coincidental" beauty, are absolutely essential to our optimal listening health since they are among the high-frequency sounds we need to best charge our brains. Some listening purists, in fact, will listen to no music that was not recorded with acoustic instruments, fearing the loss of their natural overtones.

I share Pythagoras' amazement at the orderliness and natural origins of music. Music is the perfect union of head and heart, of science and art, of will and emotion, of man and nature.

## Music as a Carrier of Intentionality

Is music truly love in search of a word? Ambrose Bierce's quote that starts this chapter is delightfully rhapsodic, depicting music as science losing its head in song, making its way to union with the soul. But where does the rhapsodic meet the road, so to speak? Is there substance beyond this gentle poetry? Most definitely. If we understand this, we can understand, appreciate, produce, and apply music in its highest, most ennobling expression.

As with all things, music is composed for deliberate purposes. The high notes of the aria sung at Mimi's death in La Boheme remains one of the most powerful energetic depictions of sorrow ever conveyed in art. The melody of "Yesterday," which came to Paul McCartney in a dream and seemed to him so exquisite that it must have been something he'd heard sometime before, conveyed a delicious sense of romanticism. And the urban drive of rap musicians such as Eminem pointedly carries the fury and frustration of a disenfranchised generation.

The intention behind how a piece of music is written, and performed, is no less important in choosing music for specific purposes than its psychoacoustic properties; in most situations, it is the most important factor. It is beyond the scope of this chapter to detail how intentionality becomes fused in the actual music of a piece, integrated into it below the more obvious level of the lyrics, though the topic is immensely fascinating. Our point here is to remind the purposeful user of music that intentionality is always present. Choose music carefully for the particular need at hand. I'm not saying censor the music. I'm saying pick pieces that appropriately support the situation. If your students are doing a presentation on the history of slavery, for example, it's entirely useful to use field hollers, the earliest tunes sung by slaves at work, and songs that convey the awful sense of human denigration. One can use compositions that reflect the human condition of a time and place. But keep such selections in perspective; one does not want to leave people dangling in the despair of a challenging time. Balance it with music that carries intentionality of hope and promise.

Music is, in the end, a mirror of human pain and growth. Nature reminds us constantly, in psychoacoustics, its natural origins, and its profound capacity to carry emotional intention, that we are inextricably connected to all things around us and to each other. Let us learn from music and consciously, carefully use it for its most benign and healing properties.

# What Skills Will Students Need for the 21$^{st}$ Century?

Ted McCain

tcpd2020@aol.com

*The material in this chapter is excerpted from a new book by the author, Teaching for Tomorrow, published by Corwin Press, 2003.*

The sweeping changes of the last thirty years have been driven by unprecedented technological development. But more than giving us new electronic toys to play with, this technological development has altered the very nature of how life is experienced. Instead of the stability of the 20$^{th}$ century, in the early 21$^{st}$ century we increasingly have to deal with change. The rate of change is now such that some say it is like living life on fast forward. The technology in the computer you take home today is obsolete before you buy it. Computer software needs continual upgrading to remain usable. Just when you get used to accessing the Internet one way, along comes a newer, faster way to do it. Bank branches are being replaced with online services, encyclopedias have moved from paper-based editions to CD ROMs to Internet sites, cell phones are letting people do everything from e-mail to taking photos to conducting business meetings. The examples of change go on and on.

This fundamental change in modern life is presenting educators with the challenge of keeping instruction relevant for their students. What skills will students need to be successful in this changing world of the 21st century? It is easy to see that the level of technology people will use in the future is only going to increase so it is logical to assume that technology skills will be critical for success. Certainly this has been a major focus in education over the last fifteen years. However, technology skills are not enough if we hope to prepare students for real success after they leave the school system. Technology skills are, in fact, secondary in importance to problem-solving skills. I learned this the hard way in my early twenties. I had an impressive set of technology skills when I left university with a degree in computer cartography. When I got a job with a mapping company looking at using a computer in their business, I thought I was perfectly suited to the position. However, once I got the job and I encountered my first real-world problems to solve, I was shocked to discover that I didn't have the thinking skills needed to do well in the world of work. I had lots of schooling, but little ability in applying my learning. I was a "Highly Educated Useless Person," very skilled in doing school-related tasks, but lacking in the abilities necessary to solve problems independently in a real-world environment. The fact that I was a "techno-wiz" with all kinds of computer skills didn't amount to a hill of beans when it came to being successful in that job.

What students really need is an education that equips them with the higher level thinking skills necessary to solve real-world problems. Unfortunately, this is something that we do not do well in the school system. We have an over-emphasis on low level thinking required to recall facts for reports and tests. If we want to prepare students for the world they will encounter when they leave the school system, then we need to rethink how we teach. And this means doing more than just adding technology instruction to our teaching load. We need to refocus on teaching that will foster independent thinking skills. I believe there are six changes we must make to our instructional approach if we want to equip our students with these critical skills.

## 1. We must resist the temptation to "tell."

As students progress through elementary school, they begin to do more serious work in terms of reports and tests. Along with this move towards more serious schoolwork comes a shift in the way children are taught. Instead of discovery learning experiences, they are increasingly told what they need to know by their teachers. They really hit this new way of teaching in junior high school (grades 8 through 10). Learning is no longer fun, it is serious business and their role is to sit and listen to their teachers tell them things.

The problem with telling is that it takes the excitement of discovery out of learning. Life is an adventure and finding out what makes it tick should be a wonderfully interesting endeavor. Telling someone something removes the first hand experience. Just think what it would be like to see a suspense movie without knowing anything about the plot. The experience of watching the actors narrowly escape certain death while the music creates a suspenseful atmosphere would get your heart pumping as you sit on the edge of your seat waiting to see if they make it through the ordeal safely. The experience would be indelibly etched in your mind. But what would your experience be if before you saw the movie, someone told you what was going to happen and that they all made it through without a scratch? Would you sit on the edge of your seat waiting to see what would happen next or would knowing the ending ruin any suspense you might have felt? That is the problem with "telling." It removes the suspense. When it comes to learning, telling does the same thing. For the vast majority of students, telling takes the fun of discovery out of learning.

Why is discovery so important? Because it generates interest in learning and interest is critical to learning. In his book, "Information Anxiety," Richard Saul Wurman captured the essential role of interest in learning when he wrote the following:

"Learning can be seen as the acquisition of information. But before it can take place, there must be interest. Interest permeates all endeavors and precedes learning. In order to acquire and remember new knowledge, it must stimulate your curiosity in some way."

Wurman goes on to say that giving students content without generating any interest in the material is like having only one side of a piece of Velcro - it just doesn't stick. I like that analogy. I believe the chief role we have as teachers is to generate interest in the material we must teach. It is our job to create the other side of the Velcro so the learning will stick in the minds of our students. This is no easy task. Some of the material we must cover is dry and learning it can be tedious. Making this course content interesting can tax all of a teacher's expertise and ingenuity. A teacher must use creativity and imagination to generate the interest needed to make instruction more palatable for their students.

## 2. We must stop teaching de-contextualized content.

Students often remark, "Why do I have to learn this?" Often teachers aren't sure why students have to learn something, either. Telling students that this is the next section in the curriculum guide isn't exactly persuasive. Students often do not see any relevance of the learning they have to do in school to the rest of their lives. Whatever the reason, many teachers do not spend the time and effort required to relate the learning being done in the classroom to real-world situations. We are experts at giving theory without providing a context. We can cover a curriculum, even test the recall of the material, but we often don't equip students with anything more than the ability to regurgitate meaningless facts. We carry the big stick of the test that forces students to work their way through the material to be covered, but student learning can be incredibly low level.

Think back to when you first heard about a significant development in sports or world events. Or think back to a significant event in your personal life like when you proposed marriage, when you learned of the death of a family member, or when you son or daughter took their first steps. Most of you will find that not only can you remember the specific event, but you can also remember the circumstances of where you were and what you were doing when it happened. Why can you remember the specifics of what you were doing that day when you have forgotten so many others? The reason is that the context of the significant event provided a frame of reference for remembering the specific information about what you were doing at that moment long after the event. This holds great promise for educators when they are attempting to get students to remember information. By providing a context for the new information, teachers are actually helping students with long-term memory. This power of context to assist with learning is worthy of note for those teachers who are struggling with preparing students for large standardized tests. By providing a context for the information, teachers are actually helping students learn the material so their recall will be better when they write the test. In addition and more importantly, context will help students with their long-term memory.

Without asking students to apply their learning to actual situations, they do not develop the skill of transferring school learning to life. Thus, it is important that we begin to make a real-world link in our teaching. This will have two major benefits. First, students will begin to develop real-world thinking skills because they are tackling the kinds of tasks they will encounter when they leave school. Second, students will also find the task of learning more interesting because they can see that the tasks they work on in school have more relevance to their life, even if it will be a few years before they completely enter that life outside school. A real-world context for learning is a key to engaging instruction.

### 3. We must stop giving students the final product of our thinking.

I remember teaching Mathematics in my first year of teaching. One day I had to do a proof of a mathematical concept on the board for my students. The proof took a few minutes to do. I was feeling very good about myself as I stopped and explained how the various steps of the proof worked. I felt sure the students were impressed with my mathematical ability. Then the wheels fell off! I reached the end of the proof and it did not work out. I felt humiliated. What do you think I did about this situation? I went home and I worked on that proof over and over again until I could do it forwards and backwards without a hitch. The next time I saw my Math class I did the proof flawlessly and I felt much better about myself. However, I have come to see a great flaw in this approach. I actually made the learning unreachable because I had done all my thinking and learning behind closed doors. All I showed my students was the final product of all my hard work. They never saw all the sweat that went into acquiring the skill that I demonstrated the second time I saw them. They never saw the multiple times I went through the proof. They never saw the trial and error approach I followed when I encountered difficulties. They never saw the messy nature of raw thinking that takes place when we are struggling to learn and solve problems. By simply showing the final result of my thinking and learning process, I made it impossible for all but the mathematically gifted students in my class to be successful.

When I realized the error in my approach, I began to look at the way we teach students in general. I believe that many teachers fall into the same trap of doing all the thinking for their students behind closed doors. When students get a work sheet, who picked the topic for the exercise? Who decided what questions to ask? When we give students a report to do, who did all the work in thinking up the project? Who decided that one section would be worth more marks than the other? Who determined the rationale for including some information and excluding other content? Who decided where the students would find the information? Now of course students need scaffolding to help them as they do their work so some structure and guidance is needed when we give them work to do. But is it possible that in the name of expediency we do much more than we should if we want them to develop independent thinking skills?

If we want to develop independence, then it is important that we start giving over some of the decision-making responsibility to our students. That means we must resist the temptation to do the work for students. It means we must place the priority on learning over expediency.

**4. We must make a fundamental shift - problems first, teaching second.**


How do tasks and problems come to us in the daily life we experience in our personal and professional lives? Does someone outline all of the parameters and specifications for us? Does someone do the initial research for where the resources are located for solving this problem? Does someone break the task down into more easily handled sub-sections? Of course not, but that is exactly what we do for students every day. And I don't mean just for the younger ones - I have seen assignments given to senior high school students where all the groundwork was done and laid out for them on the assignment sheet. All the students had to do was fill in the blanks. Presenting students with all of this groundwork done is like giving them the answer before giving them the question. Over half the work of developing the solution to a problem is already done by the teacher before the students are involved. The teacher has decided the order of the questions, the priority of points in the material, and the information to be ignored. In short, the teacher has done all of the work of defining the problem and laid it out on a piece of paper.


However, real-world problems do not come with the task neatly outlined on a printed sheet of paper. They come to us in conversations with our boss or co-workers. Problems are revealed as we are following the steps of some manufacturing process. They dawn on us as we encounter inefficiencies in the way goods are moved or people are handled. Problems are presented to us when talking to our clients who have real needs as they go about their daily business. Real-world problems are discovered in roundabout incidental ways much more than they are given to us already thought out and neatly packaged. It dawned on me that I needed to present students with problems in the same way - as incomplete statements of tasks to be done where the students must do some detective work to discover the true nature of the problem. It is critical that we begin to model the way problems and tasks come to people in the world outside school if we want students to develop the skills necessary for survival in a world without worksheets and project outlines.

## 5. We must progressively withdraw from helping students.

I believe that our focus on memorizing content in school today leads to an unrealistic emphasis on right/wrong questions in our instruction and on our tests. Students learn that it is bad to get a wrong answer. I am continually amazed at the senior students in my classes who are constantly asking me if they have the "right" answer or if their thinking is following the "right'" track. They seem incapable of working with any uncertainty for fear of being wrong. The fear of being wrong has made them dependent on their teachers. The problem is that the world outside school is an uncertain and ambiguous place with no one to tell you what to do. Often there is no right way to do something. Many major decisions are based on shaky and incomplete information where the only way to proceed is by making your best guess. Just think about buying a house. There is never any guarantee which way interest rates will go, whether you'll get the raise at work you've been counting on so you can afford a higher mortgage payment, whether a new transit line will come through the neighborhood, whether a developer will buy up the land across the street and build an apartment building, and on and on. The only way you can proceed is to do the research and then make your decision on your best assessment of where things are headed. It is the same thing with starting a new business, creating a new product, hiring a new employee - there is no guarantee, no right or wrong answer. The right/wrong approach that we use so frequently in school leads students to believe the world will be that way when they leave us. It is one of the reasons students have such a difficult time adjusting to life after school. The reality they face is much different than the world they are leaving. Unwittingly, with the best of intentions, we are preparing students for a world that does not exist. Worse, overcoming the dependence on teachers students develop in school can be an embarrassing and debilitating habit when they enter the working world.

So how do we foster independence in students? We need to learn to let go. Think back to when your children or the children of someone you know first learned to walk. Even though the child had unstable legs and a poor sense of balance, the only way they were going to learn to walk on their own was by the parent letting go of their hand. The parent's role was to encourage and assist until they were no longer needed. That is the approach we must adopt in teaching school. If our goal is independence, then just like a parent, our job should be to make ourselves obsolete. Students should no longer need us when they leave the school system.

## 6.     We must re-evaluate evaluation.

Currently, much of the evaluation in schools is done with written tests based on the content laid out in the standards set by a state or province. Ultimately, students write standardized tests created by the state or provincial department of education. These tests ensure that there is uniform instruction on the basic material in courses throughout the school system. However, you need more than just test scores if you want to get a complete picture of what a student has really accomplished in their schooling. Dave Master uses an analogy to make this point. His wife is a nurse and she has told him that you can get a good picture of someone's health by measuring a person's height and weight. But Master then asks if you would go to a doctor who only did those two measurements when assessing your health? Of course not. You would expect a full picture of your health to involve much more than stepping on a scale and checking how tall you are. You would want your physician to check your heart rate, measure your blood pressure, check your cholesterol, check your white blood cell count, check your eye sight, do a complete urine analysis, check your body for areas of pain or discomfort, feel for unusual lumps, check your hearing, listen to your breathing, and perform a myriad of other tests depending on your age and any unusual symptoms they found. Only then could the doctor have a full picture of your health and only then could you have confidence in what he or she had to say. In the same way, we must measure student learning in multiple ways if we hope to get a complete picture of student performance. Written tests have their place in assessing learning, but it is important that we truly consider what a particular evaluative tool is measuring. It is quite possible to place too much stock in what learning a test actually checks.

I have a great concern that the emphasis on written testing as the chief means for evaluation is leading to a very narrow view of what learning is and how that learning is demonstrated. While written tests have their place, they only give part of the picture. There are a number of other ways for students to demonstrate what they have learned. Teachers can evaluate portfolios of student work. Students can demonstrate their ability to perform certain tasks in timed exercises. Students can do real-world work - create a web site for a company, build a desk, publish a magazine, cater a banquet, write and produce a play, do a small house renovation. However, having students do these kinds of activities seems to be lessening, not increasing, in schools today. What I find most disturbing about a focus on content standards and standardized testing is that the evaluative tail is wagging the instructional dog in education. In other words, because performance on tests based on content standards is the only measurement that is given real meaning in assessing a student's learning, instruction in other skill areas is actually dropping because it takes time away from what is being measured. This is of great concern because performance on standardized tests is a school skill that does not transfer to the real-world environment. I see students leaving high school today who have great ability to perform on tests who would not be able to hold a job because they couldn't problem-solve their way out of a wet paper bag.

## Conclusion

What skills will students need to be successful in the 21$^{st}$ century? Certainly much of what we now teach in school will remain important in educating young people. This includes teaching such things as mastering reading for information and enjoyment, learning to communicate well through writing and other media, being able to compute and calculate, understanding the social and political implications of history, geography and government, and being able to utilize the power of new technologies. But the critical skills students will need for success in the future are the thinking skills that revolve around the ability to solve real-world problems independently. Unfortunately, teaching students to problem-solve on their own on tasks that relate to the world outside school is something we do not do very well in education today.

In this brief commentary, I have outlined six changes I believe are necessary to engender the independent problem-solving skills our students will need for success in the future. They are:

1. Resist the temptation to tell (rather, provide opportunities for students to engage in discovery learning);

2. Stop teaching de-contextualized content (rather, make obvious the relevance of everything we're teaching to life beyond school);

3. Stop giving students the final product of our thinking (rather, make learning a priority over expedience so that students have time and encouragement to explore ideas);

4. Put problems first, teaching second (that is, model how problems come to people in the real world, and give students opportunities to experience approaching and thinking through problems and solutions);

5. Progressively withdraw from helping students (that is, celebrate "wrong" answers as a means to solving problems so that students can excel on their own without us when they leave school); and finally,

6. Re-evaluate evaluation (that is, recognize that standardized tests give a very narrow picture of what students know, and work on developing a complete picture through a variety of evaluation strategies).

For our students to be truly successful with this new approach, we will need to adjust our instruction to include teaching students the process to follow when they encounter new problems. I have developed an approach called the 4 D's that embodies the essential steps one must follow to solve any problem. However, a discussion of that process is beyond the scope of this publication.

By implementing these ideas into our teaching, we will see students take more responsibility for their learning. Further, using this new approach, we will re-discover the reasons we first became teachers: to share the excitement of discovery with students, and continue our own learning as they create solutions beyond our own thinking.

# Using Data-Driven Dialogues to Increase the Speed, Breadth and Depth of Student Results

Bernajean Porter

tcpd2020@aol.com

*When a living system is confronted by new information, and when this new information builds to a certain level of intensity, it creates a disturbance so large that the system no longer remains stable. It jars the system out of its current form.*

– Margaret Wheatley, *Leadership and the New Science* (1992).

What is the role of technology in transforming and accelerating our schools into systems capable of educating students for success careers in a 21$^{st}$ century economy? How will we scale and sustain the unique benefits generated by technology pilot projects for ALL students? What influence can data collections have on these questions as a team grapples with the planning, implementation, and accountability of our technology resources to maximize the possible impact on student results?

The work we have ahead of us is not just about the data collection tools, although we can be thankful for all the national efforts to generate the assessment instruments that we now need. It is about HOW we use the data and tools to educate and mobilize our systems to act in the highest interest of our students' lives. After surveys, interviews or inventory counts have been given, then what? What purposes and results do you expect for the effort and cost of gathering this data? How will you know if the data collection process has been worth the time and dollar resources it took?

*Accountability means everyone taking responsibility for deciding first what they want to have happen for their students (vision and goals) NOT possible without the technical tools, and then using data to direct and redirect all resources to have the maximum effect possible on those outcomes for all students.*

First, are you measuring for efforts or results? Efforts include buying and installing equipment, training a designated number of staff for a certain number of hours, or assigning students to do two or more projects a year with technology. For example, asking teachers to "integrate throughout the curriculum" is an effort goal. Many learning goals created for technology plans were intentionally broad and general so as not to step directly on any curriculum group's territory. Goals were couched in general terms such as "enriching or enhancing curriculum," "creating lifelong learners," "supporting state standards," or "integrating technology throughout the curriculum." Though these sound like worthy goals, when it comes to evaluating these outcomes we are actually left with counting the ITs-instructional technology activities. For example, would assessing for these goals each year entail measuring for the percentage of teachers doing three "enrichings" and two "enhancings," or using four out of any of the 300 standards, or completing two "integrations"? When broad learning goals are used in plans, teachers are left "to do what they want, do what they can, but use IT somehow." When put to the demand of assessment, the vagueness of the language only leaves the ability to count the efforts. With broad, undefined goals guiding implementation, the context of the learning culture remains unchallenged and unchanged even though technology varies or enhances student learning. Results cannot be developed with optional budgets, optional technical support, optional student uses, and optional staff development.

When implementation goals are organized around efforts, data collections are generally about counting things. Measuring the progress of efforts can be done by using quantitative data tools: tracking inventories, connectivity, budgets, hours of access, number of student uses as well as giving surveys on attitudes, uses and skills.

On the other hand, if you want to develop accountability for added-value results, goals need to be directly about student learning outcomes not hardware acquisition and adults needs or uses. Results are considered to be the measurable changes and benefits that students experience because of the efforts that were made. Three essential elements are needed to obtain results: specific, measurable learning goals; performance data; and team work. (Schmoker, *Results: the Key to continuous School Improvement*, 1996). Specific, measurable learning goals, rather than effort goals, now organize the best and worth-the-money exemplary student uses of technology in schools for all students. Varied and strategic data collection becomes essential to guide and document the success of the implementation work for results.

*Relying only upon single source data like surveys can actually misdirect the implementation efforts in ways that not only waste resources but may even inhibit reaching designated goals!*

Measuring for results requires data to combine qualitative as well as quantitative sources of information that can be triangulated for dependable decision-making. (Triangulation of findings is the use of at least three or more types of data from multiple sources - both qualitative and quantitative data - to reach valid conclusions.) Three varied sources of data pointing to the same conclusion negates the bias of any single type of data collection, such as self-reported surveys.

Quantitative data by itself will never be able to tell the whole story of student results. Data collections for results will need to include artifact analysis (lesson plans, curriculum documents, staff development documents), multiple group surveys, interviews, building observations of student uses and instructional tasks, and finally gathering student work as instructional evidence to create a comprehensive force-field analysis. Beware of using single source data collections like surveys to guide implementation resources and decisions if you are measuring for results! Relying only upon surveys can actually misdirect the implementation efforts in ways that not only waste resources but may even inhibit reaching designated goals. Evaluation of results requires varied and multiple sources of data to ensure validity of findings in order for next decisions to actually increase results for students.

Developing a force-field analysis is a system process used to identify what's working and what needs to work better to overcome any barriers that might prohibit success. The more stakeholders who participate in developing the force-field analysis, the more ownership of the situation AND the more the ownership of the solutions increases. Evaluating for results is not just about having data but about continually using data to educate and mobilize our schools to ensure that technology's potential is activated for all students.

*The goal is not having data; it is to develop "catalytic validity." This is "the degree to which the research energizes participants toward knowing reality in order to transform it."* (Gary Anderson *et al.*, Studying Your Own School, 1994).

Are we ready to shift from an effort approach to data collections to a results approach to data collections - from optional language in our effort goals to essential uses developed with specific, measurable goals - from the disparity of student experiences to taking responsibility for delivering what all students have a right to experience? If schools are ready for these shifts, they will need to realize that a simplistic approach to data solutions will inhibit and possibly even misdirect their ability to implement the education technology vision for all students. When shifting into accountability for results, valid information is intentionally used to educate and mobilize the school system to take action. There is an urgent need to embrace and fund a comprehensive approach to the data collection, using multiple data tools along with group processes as a vehicle for educating and mobilizing our system to take action.

*It isn't the data . . . it is what you do with the data that make the real difference.*

I have dedicated my own work with assessment these past eight years to Fernando Flores' words that "an organization's results are determined through webs of human commitments born in webs of human conversations." Lipton and Wellman's work, *Delving into Data* (2000), expand on Flores' point by incorporating group processes with the use of data. Data by itself has no meaning. It is simply information. Meaning can only be made by the individuals and groups who work TOGETHER to interpret the information through their own frames of reference. Dialogue makes possible a flow of meaning in a group, out which emerges new understanding now possible because of the diverse perspectives. Lipton and Wellman make a distinction between data-driven dialogues, which promotes organizational learning and collective action, and the current movement to organize data-driven decisions. Dialogue that leads to collaborative planning and problem-solving actions is not the same approach as what is commonly presented as data-driven decision making. Data-driven decision-making does not usually incorporate collective processes to involve stakeholders. However, it is the engagement and involvement of people in the group processes that enable a system to transform itself to the next levels of possibility.

*The speed, breadth, and depth of change is directly connected to number of stakeholders who own the situation and also own the urgency of generating solutions to move forward.* (Robert Jacobs, *Real Time Strategic Change*, 1994).

If we are to mobilize our systems to address the technology issues of scalability, equity and accountability, our data collection processes need to involve a large group of stakeholders in making sense of the data, owning the problem/situation and then . . .developing urgent action items that will mobilize what needs to happen next to increase the speed and depth of what is really possible for students.

I am committed to facilitating assessment processes with schools that not only collects data but also includes group processes like member checking of the data, feedback loops with multiple stakeholders, and finally a strategic retreat involving leadership teams in prioritizing and determining next steps based on the data. The two-day strategy retreat is a closing event in the data collection process that brings together a broad group of stakeholders to consider the data, prioritize actions needed to move forward and then to collectively develop work plans to make the changes needed for more results. Schools are human institutions, not easily governed by the logic of numbers and the curve of percentages. Data-driven dialogue throughout the assessment process engenders changes in the organization by supporting groups in inquiry, reflection, and finally continuous generation of implementation strategies that move **everyone** in the system forward.

In conclusion, let me say that I have found very few schools presently organized for the accountability issues focusing on technology integration that are being raised in our communities today. Between the installation of equipment and the delivery of student results there exists another step that is often overlooked and certainly underrated. The entire school system (parents, teachers, principals, school board and community members) needs to take mutual responsibility to intentionally organize itself to collectively target and deliver learning results for all students - that is accountability!

Too much of our technology use is still optional with an over emphasis on technical efforts and uses. Too many evaluation projects and planning projects attempt to grapple with the expectation to demonstrate accountability when implementation is organized around optional, unfocused student uses of technology; optional budgets using whatever money is available; optional expectations for results; optional staff development events; optional technical support - even optional equipment distribution ratios for students. Accountability is desirable but not likely to be possible with optional and unfocused efforts. Technology resources need to be used more effectively to alter and accelerate designated classroom practices not limited to simplistic check-lists for demonstrating technology skills. Many schools have good things happening that will not happen for all students without some concerted effort to do so. Meaningful quantitative AND qualitative data-dialogues can accelerate the decisions needed to speed up visible results.

Technology creates a level of perturbation that demands significant changes in school culture if technology is to truly add value to what schools accomplish! Many political and local groups are ready to eliminate whatever seems extra or is not understood to be serving our student's highest needs. As long as the results from student uses of our technology resources are not understood or valued, future funding and support will be questionable. The question is not, "What has technology done for education?" Rather, it is "What can technology do for our kids if we consciously use the power of technology to reorganize, reshape and accelerate our schools in ways that prepare students to thrive in a changing, complex world?" There has always been magic in communities working together to make good things happen for kids. Combining a comprehensive data collection with facilitated group data-dialogue processes will increase the speed, breadth, and depth of targeted results for **all** students.

# Contemporary Literacy in the Digital Age: From Vision to Strategy

Ferdi Serim

tcpd2020@aol.com

*The material in this chapter is excerpted from a book by the author, Information Technology for Learning: No School Left Behind, published by Big6 Associates, 2003.*

Technology is the Big Bang that has propelled literacy into an expanding universe. Scientists, no longer able to keep up through printed journals, now understand each other's work online, using sophisticated visualizations and simulations made possible by supercomputing. Economists, unable to process the volume and complexity of financial transactions, employ armies of programmers to deploy powerful tools for real-time visualization of the flow of wealth. Visualization extends literacy by enabling people to perceive relationships hidden below the surface of vast amounts of data, and to synthesize meaning from these relationships. The challenge for "everyday people" to keep up with this expansion can only be met through development of Information & Communications Technology (ICT) Literacy, because information "thinking skills" are the true essential skills for the 21$^{st}$ Century.

As we seek 21$^{st}$ Century skills for our students, we must develop (and model) these ourselves. If we want to elevate the levels of student performance, we also need to elevate the levels of tasks they are given. As educators, our task is to shape the system so that it reflects the needs of learners (both students and teachers). Some of this work we do with teachers, some with school leaders, and some with our communities. This new work is way beyond the boundaries defining the education profession in the past century.

Until the public understands what learning in the 21$^{st}$ century looks like, translating goals into policy and practice will remain elusive. Decisions made at all levels are pulled back into the gravitational sphere of the familiar. The resulting inertia reinforces existing practice rather than seizing opportunities to redirect time, talent, and resources to develop skills required by students, parents, and communities to fully participate in contemporary life. Although the needs of different stakeholders (government, business, education, communities) vary, communicating a common vision of what is possible allows each group to make choices and contributions that lead to effective actions. I've coined the term "Contemporary Literacy" to help us see the components as a coherent whole.

## Walking the Talk into the Digital Age

Archimedes said, "Give me a place to stand, and I can move the world." One powerful idea provides us with a location for such leverage, and that is collaboration. When collaboration is combined with information literacy and critical thinking, it can transform the communities within which our professional lives unfold.

As a classroom teacher, when I began to introduce the mind-boggling array of resources that the Internet provided to my students, I quickly found that my professional preparation had neglected crucial concepts and skills. Unlike many of my peers, technology wasn't a hang-up, since I'd worked as a systems analyst before returning to teaching. Like almost all of my peers, I was forced to rely on intuition and luck in terms of finding, evaluating, managing, organizing, and presenting the increasingly small proportion of truly useful information the Internet was shining on my mind. It turns out that these very skills are what my colleagues who went to library school had mastered.

Collaborating and conversing with peers, both face to face and within online communities of practice, I began to see parallel gaps:

- People who spent their professional lives creating clearinghouses wondered why education didn't suddenly improve in the presence of vastly superior information

- People who devoted their talents and energies to improving speed and bandwidth of the networks available to learners wondered why there wasn't a commensurate leap in quality of student projects.

It seemed that as educators, we had all the puzzle pieces without the box top picture to help us put things together in a meaningful way.

The single most elusive element was the answer to the question, "Why bother?" The vast amounts of investment in money, time, and talent required to make technology commonplace in classrooms seemed like an idea searching for justification, instead of a natural outcome of the pursuit of educational excellence.

It has become clear to me that each of us confronts a locked gate, for which someone else holds the key. Moreover, we each have keys for doors we no longer find locked. By communicating and collaborating, we can work our way out of the funhouse distortions that help us distinguish school from "real life."

It has further become clear to me that the Information Literacy Standards, taken together with ISTE's National Education Technology Standards, provide us with the common ground from which we can move the education world from its troubled slumber into the wakefulness of contemporary reality. Although learning never stops, many of us experience this moment as a new beginning, when we reach out across traditional boundaries and build a foundation from which we can move into the kind of world we'd like to inhabit. Contemporary Literacy provides us with the lever to focus the force to "make it so."

**What Is Contemporary Literacy?**
Contemporary Literacy involves much more than the reading and writing of text. It includes hypertext writing, visual thinking and information-based problem solving. As veteran educator and information specialist Janet Murray says, "This connotation of 'literacy' - one that includes interpretation and evaluation of a medium of expression - has been applied in many different contexts. We read about visual literacy, media literacy, textual literacy, numerical literacy, technology literacy, and network literacy. In each case, the author expects the word 'literacy' to suggest a

complex of skills, including analysis, evaluation, synthesis, and application." Moreover, implementing a program of contemporary literacy generates digital educational evidence for decision-making at the school and classroom level, allowing schools to move beyond the practice of education as an "evidence-free zone."

As noted in the 1999 National Research Council report *Being Fluent with Information Technology*, (National Research Council, 1999) the "requirement of a deeper understanding than is implied by the rudimentary term 'computer literacy' motivated the committee to adopt 'fluency' as a term connoting a higher level of competency. People fluent with information technology (FIT persons) are able to express themselves creatively, to reformulate knowledge, and to synthesize new information. Fluency with information technology (i.e., what this report calls FITness) entails a process of lifelong learning in which individuals continually apply what they know to adapt to change and acquire more knowledge to be more effective at applying information technology to their work and personal lives."

As we develop measures of these skills, we need to recognize both the context, as well as the nature of the process, and how this process differs from those typically measured in schools. The report notes, "Because FITness is fundamentally integrative, calling upon an individual to coordinate information and skills with respect to multiple dimensions of a problem and to make overall judgments and decisions taking all such information into account, a project-based approach to developing FITness is most appropriate."

In January 2001, Educational Testing Service (ETS) convened an international panel to study the growing importance of existing and emerging Information and Communication Technologies (ICT) and their relationship to literacy. Their report, *Digital Transformation*, (ETS, 2002) puts forth a framework that defines ICT literacy as "using digital technology, communications tools, and/or networks to access, manage, integrate, evaluate, and create information in order to function in a knowledge society." (A free PDF copy of this report is available at http://www.ets.org/research/ictliteracy/ictreport.pdf)

The panel found that "ICT literacy cannot be defined primarily as the mastery of technical skills. The panel concludes that the concept of ICT literacy should be broadened to include both critical cognitive skills as well as the application of technical skills and knowledge. These cognitive skills include general literacy, such as reading and numeracy, as well as critical thinking and problem solving. Without such skills, the panel believes that true ICT literacy cannot be attained."

Such definitions of 21$^{st}$ Century Skills heighten the importance of the work of Information & Technology (I&T) Teams at every level. Only when the people responsible for curricular, instructional, management, and technical aspects of the school operate from a shared understanding of the importance of ICT Literacy can their actions align to make contemporary literacy possible for all students.

## From Vision to Strategy

Today, it is all too easy to shift the focus from learning onto test scores. To do so is to confuse the starting line with the finish line. Certainly a mastery of the skills traditionally associated with literacy is a pre-requisite for applying the power technology brings to communication and collaboration. However, the race has yet to begin when acceptable test scores are achieved, because measurements for the skills demanded for success in the 21$^{st}$ century are not in place. Nevertheless, we assert that contemporary literacy for all teachers and students will improve student achievement and promote lifelong learning that exceeds the mandated accountability provisions of No Child Left Behind. Our vision of contemporary literacy both incorporates information literacy and builds on traditional literacy. Our vision of contemporary literacy embraces not only computers and data, but also includes the critical thinking skills required to use them effectively.

Educators, decision-makers, and communities require both a vision of contemporary literacy and a strategy for making the journey from this vision to practice. My research has led me to advocate the formation of Information & Technology (I&T) Teams at the building level, in order to provide the capacity for sustained support of educational improvement. The members of the I&T Team are the people in schools who are most involved in the redesign of learning to reflect contemporary realities: the principal, the library media specialist, the teacher leader, and the technical specialist (supported by the District Technology Coordinator). Note, we don't say support for technology: the efforts must remain firmly fixed on the goal of improved learning, through system wide improvement at the school level, with the role of technology clearly as servant rather than master.

I've found these analogies to be most useful in helping people understand the roles of the members of the I&T Team:

**Wizard -** the person who knows about managing systems and processes for technology at the district level. [District Chief Technology Officer]

**Pilot -** the person who knows about managing people, schedules and budgets at the building level. [Principal]

**Scholar -** the person who knows about locating information and organizing knowledge. [Library/Media Specialist]

**Guide -** the person who knows about designing and implementing learning experiences, and has the most daily contact with a particular set of children. [Teacher Leader]

**Hard Hat -** the person who knows about making hardware, software, and networks function. [Technical Specialist]


**Every Strategy Needs a Process**

In December 2000, *e-Learning: Putting a World Class Education at the Fingertips of All Children*, (U.S. Dept. Of Ed., 2000) the second National Technology Plan ever devised was released. In addressing ICT Literacy, the plan states, "A meaningful, unified approach to providing students with the skills they will need for their futures must be more than a checklist of isolated technology skills, such as knowing the parts of a computer, writing drafts and final products with a word processor, or searching for information using a CD-ROM database.

"Rather, technology skills are only a first step in assuring all our children become proficient information and technology users. Also necessary are information literacy skills such as:

- *Task definition* - The first step in the information problem-solving process is to recognize that an information need exists, to define the problem, and to identify the types and extent of information needed.
- *Information seeking strategies* - Once the information problem has been formulated, the student must consider all possible information sources and develop a plan for searching.
- *Location and access* - After students determine their priorities for information seeking, they must locate information from a variety of resources, access specific information found within individual resources, and evaluate the quality of resources.

- *Use of information* - After finding potentially useful resources, students must engage (read, view, listen) the information to determine its relevance and then extract the relevant information.
- *Synthesis* - Students must organize and communicate the results of the information problem-solving effort.
- *Evaluation* - Evaluation focuses on how well the product meets the original task (effectiveness) and the process of how well students carried out the problem-solving process (efficiency)."

**Information Literacy: The Key to Evidence Based Practice**

The plan described above is the Big6 Approach to Information Problem Solving, the most widely known and used approach to teaching information and technology skills. Given the new national educational policy focus on improving student achievement, through research-based practices which document student growth, the Big6 contribution to the work of developing 21st Century Skills is both timely and imperative. Meeting the research challenges of No Child Left Behind is best understood as a Knowledge Management problem. It's not that individuals in the system don't have access to information; it's that the system is not structured to apply the knowledge it "owns" in the form of the Intellectual Capital of its constituents. Even with access to the best research, and the best designed processes for collecting student/program performance data, schools would still need to learn how to transfer this knowledge into the real-world classroom settings where improved student achievement actually occurs.

To assist school leaders in meeting this Knowledge Management problem, I've had success using the Big6, which provides a systematic process based on six broad skill areas necessary for successful information problem-solving. This approach builds a set of skills and an organized strategy for effectively meeting information needs while developing critical thinking skills.

The research basis for this approach is extensive. In her recent literature review of this research, (Lowe, 2002) Carrie Lowe writes, "Information literacy is not a set of individual tasks or skills, but rather a way of thinking that allows individuals to be the flexible thinkers and lifelong learners who will succeed in the information age." Regarding the value of information literacy, Lowe notes that the cognitive aspects and related benefits are key. "Pitts' (1995) examination of the mental models of students engaged in the information problem-solving process found that they use different domains of knowledge to complete a task, including one responsible for information seeking and use, and others related to the other aspects of the task, including subject knowledge. Pitts found that a lack of knowledge in one area (including information problem-solving skills) could limit learning and success overall."

The crucial importance of ICT Literacy heightens the value of successful implementations. Lowe reports, "Eisenberg and Berkowitz (1988) found that the best way to teach information literacy skills (such as the Big6) in curriculum context is through the collaboration of classroom teachers and library media specialists. Brievik (1998) found that the same is true in higher education, as students succeed in integrated courses designed by faculty members and academic librarians."

This is precisely the approach taken by thousands of educators as they work with their colleagues in applying the Big6 Skills to their instruction and assessment. The cover story for MultiMedia Schools magazine May/June 2002 issue, *Moving Every Child Ahead: the Big6 Success Strategy*, describes how this powerful ICT strategy has resulted in improved student achievement for several years running. Instead of teaching to the test, scores are raised by improving

102

student thinking skills. (See http://www.infotoday.com/MMSchools/may02/berkowitz.htm)

**Contemporary Literacy: Moving Every Child Ahead**
In Seattle (June 2002), at ThinkQuest Live! Exploring the Future of Learning, Terry Rogers, developer of the Exploring the Future of Learning initiative, issued the following challenge:

"By the year 2010 children will have access to a working and cost effective learning environment adapted to their individual learning aptitudes and goals, which is as compelling as other parts of their environment, and which helps them achieve their full potential in the world and which is capable of being adapted and used worldwide."

Meanwhile, across the country in Washington, DC, the US Department of Education clarified the regulations that states will follow to make sure that no child is left behind. Both of these noble and inspiring efforts add dimensions to our work in real classrooms and in real schools that go beyond anything we've known before. While much remains to be determined relative to which pathways will prove most effective, it is not too early to say that the answers will emerge from the local level, rather than as pronouncements from inside the Beltway. In the quest for evidence based practice, our classrooms become the living laboratories for studied interventions. Our skills in facilitating research and project-based learning are often overlooked by decision makers at all levels, but are critical to the success of any response to the challenges of No Child Left Behind.

Schools face a set of significant challenges in bringing "the power of rigorous, objective, scientific understanding to bear on improving decisions about educational programming and thus student achievement," as stated in the law. These decisions shape fundamental questions about how schools design, implement and assess instruction to meet the needs of all children. The district and school leaders we work with require robust information about how they compare to similar districts across the country, as well as a means for communicating with their peers in their cohort about what has worked in meeting specific educational challenges. The members of the I&T Team are the professionals best equipped to lead in the transformation to evidence based practice.

So that we are not distracted by the baggage of hyperfocus on annualized, high stakes testing, or the merits of improving education by eliminating "failing schools," let's consider the characteristics shared by approaches that focus on growth rather than punishment. Let's call such an approach Moving Every Child Ahead, so as not to confuse such efforts with the legislated requirements of No Child Left Behind.

As schools across the nation grapple with the challenge to Move Every Child Ahead, the importance of research-based approaches highlights two critical needs:

- our need to find and apply the most relevant research to classroom practice

- our need to gather valid evidence through these practices, as a basis for decisions

Schools need help to accomplish the task of bridging research and practice within a context that reflects the scientific processes of inquiry. By developing district capacity for information-based problem solving, we become generators of educational evidence for decision making at the school and classroom level, allowing our schools to move beyond the practice of education as an "evidence-free zone." Educators are the first professionals who need to develop and apply contemporary literacy skills to the challenges of their work.

## Conclusion: Contemporary Literacy Requires Digital Equity

Literacy has always been at the heart of the education enterprise. From the time of the 3Rs to now, being literate has been a consistent yet evolving foundation for citizenship in each cultural era. Literacy has also been used as a wedge, from the times of slavery (when teaching slaves to read was a felony) until the Civil Rights era, when literacy tests relied upon the inequality of schools to recreate a disenfranchised population by proxy.

We are at a pivotal moment regarding education and society - a moment that challenges us to focus FITness on the process of improving education. For once, the course of action we advocate aligns with the general public's high priorities for (and deep concerns about) the direction and quality of learning provided by the public education system. When our actions are understood as a concerted effort to improve school and student performance, we can tap in to powerful community impulses to join and support this effort. We are guided by a vision for engaging "students in the learning process in order to help them attain the higher standards set for today's learners and tomorrow's leaders," a vision we share with the Baldrige Education Criteria for Performance Excellence.

The skills and capabilities required for success in the 21$^{st}$ century are embedded in the tools and tasks that comprise the I&T team's daily work. Although the elements for success exist in your school, they lie dormant until they are aligned to support the compelling vision of contemporary literacy in a digital age. We see what must be done, but the job is too big for any of us. That's why we advocate forming teams at the building level, bringing together the expertise of diverse professionals to focus their efforts in a coordinated way. Not only do we intuitively know that such a course of action is right, we are riding a wave of change that traverses all elements of society. The time to start is now, when the communities who provide context for our work in schools seem to understand the imperative that we prepare our children for the challenges and responsibilities that become theirs when they leave our care.

## References:

National Research Council (1999) *Being Fluent with Information Technology,* Committee on Information Technology Literacy, National Research Council, National Academy Press, Washington, DC 20055 http://books.nap.edu/html/beingfluent/

Educational Testing Service (2002) *Digital Transformation: A Framework for ICT Literacy* (draft) Educational Testing Service, Princeton, NJ.

U. S. Department of Education (2000) *e-Learning: Putting a World Class Education at the Fingertips of All Children,* US Dept of Education, Washington, DC.

Lowe, Carrie (2002) *Research Foundations of the Big6 Skills* http://www.big6.com/showarticle.php?id=145

Pitts, J. et al. (1995) *Mental Models of Information: The 1993-1994 AASL/Highsmith Research Award Study,* **School Library Media Quarterly, 23**(3), 177-184.

Eisenberg, M.B. and Berkowitz, R.E. (1988) *Curriculum Initiative: An Agenda and Strategy for Library Media Programs,* Worthington, OH: Linworth.

Brievik, P.S. (1998) *Student Learning in the Information Age,* Phoenix, AZ: Oryx Press.

# The Case for Computing

Gary S. Stager
tcpd2020@aol.com

The personal computer is the most powerful, expressive, and flexible instrument ever invented. At its best, the PC offers learners a rich intellectual laboratory and vehicle for self-expression. Although computing has transformed nearly every aspect of society, schools remain relatively untouched.

This chapter is not about predicting the future. It is about the learning opportunities that exist today and may be overlooked. Computers and creativity are in dangerously short supply. The dearth of compelling models of using computers in deeper ways has created a vacuum now filled by a Dickensian approach to schooling.

When I read the growing mountain of educational technology standards I can't help but wonder if these objectives could be satisfied without the use of a computer. The unimaginative use of school computers is symptomatic of larger crises in schooling, including what Seymour Papert calls "idea aversion." Over the past few decades I have enjoyed working at key moments in the intersection of learning and computers. My daily work is guided by an optimism rooted in experiences learning with computers and observing children doing the same. As much as this is the story of great promise and great disappointment, the children we serve sustain our enthusiasm to work harder to realize the learning potential of the digital age.

**Ancient History - My Early Years of Computing**

In 1976 I got to touch a computer for the first time. My junior high school (grades 6-8) had a mandatory computer-programming course for seventh and eighth graders. More than a quarter century ago, the Wayne Township Public Schools in New Jersey thought it was important for all kids to have experience programming computers. There was never any discussion of preparation for computing careers, school-to-work, presentation graphics, or computer literacy. Computer programming was viewed as a window onto a world of ideas given equal status as industrial arts, music appreciation, art, and oral communications.

The scarcity of classroom computers made programming a highly social activity since we were often leaning over each other's shoulders in order to get in on the action.

Mr. Jones, the computer programming teacher, was scary in a Dr. Frankenstein sort of way. However, I was attracted by the realization that this guy could make computers do things!

Mr. Jones knew how elaborate computer games worked and would show us the code after school if we were interested. Once I understood how to read a computer program, I could THINK LIKE THE COMPUTER! This made me feel powerful.

The feelings of intellectual elation I experienced programming are indescribable. The computer amplified my thinking. I could start with the germ of an idea and through incremental success and debugging challenges, build something more sophisticated than I could have ever imagined.

The self-awareness that I was a competent thinker helped me survive the indignities of high school mathematics classes. The ability to visualize divergent paths, anticipate bugs, and rapidly test

108

mental scenarios is the direct result of computer programming. This gift serves me in everyday life when I need to hack my way through a voicemail system to reach a knowledgeable human, or get my car out of a locked parking structure.

Perhaps Mr. Jones was such a great teacher because he was learning to program too - maybe just slightly ahead of us. (This never occurred to me as a kid, since Mr. Jones knew everything about computers.)

A strong community of practice emerged in the high school computer room. We learned from each other, challenged one another, and played with each other's programs. We altered timeshare games, added ways to cheat, and programmed cheap tricks designed to shock classmates. I even ran after school classes in BASIC for kids interested in learning to program.

Computers were to be used to make things at my high school, not as a subject of study. There was never a mention of computer literacy, and owning a computer was unthinkable. The school computers were a place to lose ourselves in powerful ideas.

We never saw a manual for a piece of software, although we treasured every issue of Creative Computing - working hard to meticulously enter hundreds of lines of computer code only to have every single program be buggy. Since we had little idea what was impossible, we thought anything was possible. We felt smart, powerful and creative. We took Fortran manuals out of the public library for no other reason than to hold a connection to a larger world of computing - a world we were inventing for ourselves.

Bill Gates and Steve Wozniak were involved in similar little ventures at the time. Many of the computing visionaries who changed the world enjoyed comparable early experiences with computers. I remember the explosion of thinking and creativity I experienced programming computers and try to recreate the spirit of that computer-rich learning culture in every school I visit. Kids deserve no less.

In the mid-80s I was welcomed into the global "Logo community" and asked to present papers at places like MIT. This was pretty heady stuff for a failed trumpet player and mediocre student. Logo programming offered a vehicle for sharing my talents, expressing my creativity and engaging in powerful ideas with some of the leading thinkers in education. Seymour Papert's scholarship gave voice to my intuitions vis-á-vis the tension between schooling and learning.

To this day, my work with adults and kids is centered around using computers as intellectual laboratories and vehicles for self-expression. To experience the full power of computing, the tools need to be flexible, extensible, and transparent. The user needs to be fluent in the grammar of the system whether it is text based, symbolic, or gestural.

**Laptops**
In 1989, Methodist Ladies' College (MLC), an Australian PK-12 school already recognized for its world-class music education, committed to every student having a personal laptop computer. By the time I began working with MLC a year later, 5th and 7th graders were required to own a laptop. The "P" in PC was taken very seriously. Personal computing would not only solve the obvious problems of student access, low levels of faculty fluency, and the costs associated with the construction of computer labs, but the PC would embody the wisdom of Dewey, Vygotsky, and Piaget. Logo, because of its open-endedness and cross-curricular potential, was the justification for ubiquitous hardware.

MLC principal, David Loader, understood that the personal was at the core of any efforts to make his school more learner-centered. He was not shy in his desire to radically reinvent his school. Bold new thinking, epistemological breakthroughs, sensitivity to a plurality of learning styles, increased collaboration (among teachers and children), and student self-reliance were expected outcomes of the high-tech investment. Teachers learning not only to use, but program, computers would acquaint themselves with the type of "hard fun" envisioned for student learning.

If the computer was to play a catalytic role in this educational shift, it was obvious that the computers needed to be personal. Truly creative and intellectual work requires freedom and a respect for privacy. Quality work is contingent on sufficient time to think, to experiment, to play. The laptop can only become an extension of the child when it is available at all times. Therefore, there was never any debate about laptops going home with students. Time and time again, the most interesting work was accomplished during the student's personal time.

The constant availability of laptops was a way to enable students to engage in programming and make constructionism concrete.

MLC was a magical place during the early nineties. Every aspect of schooling was open for discussion and reconsideration.

When I expressed concern over the gap between classroom reality and the rhetoric proclaiming the school's commitment to constructionism, the principal supported my desire to take dozens of teachers away for intensive residential professional development sessions. After all, constructionism is something you DO as well as believe. You cannot be a constructionist who subcontracts the construction. "Do as I say, not as I do" would no longer cut it.

A renaissance of learning and teaching catapulted MLC and the subsequent Australian "laptop schools" to the attention of school reformers around the world.

We were ecstatic when students began to adorn their laptops with their names written in glitter paint. This signaled appropriation. The computers mattered. Success.

The early success of MLC and the many other "laptop schools" to follow were a realization of the dream Seymour Papert and Alan Kay held for decades. In 1968, computer scientist Alan Kay visited Seymour Papert at MIT. Papert, a protégé of Jean Piaget, a mathematician and artificial intelligence pioneer was combining his interests by designing computing environments in which children could learn. Kay was so impressed by how children in Papert's Logo Lab were learning meaningful mathematics that he sketched the Dynabook, a dream of portable computers yet to be fully realized, on the flight home to Xerox PARC, a leading high-tech thinktank.

Kay set out to design a portable personal computer for children on which complex ideas could come alive through the construction of simulations. Dr. Kay recently remembered this time by saying, "More and more, I was thinking of the computer not just as hardware and software but as a medium through which you could communicate important things. Before I got involved with computers I had made a living teaching guitar. I was thinking about the aesthetic relationship people have with their musical instruments and the phrase popped into my mind: an instrument whose music is ideas." (Kay, 2003)

Kay's poetic vision resonated with my memories of Mr. Jones, summer camp, and my own experiences programming in Logo.

Kay went on to say, "One of the problems with the way computers are used in education is that they are most often just an extension of this idea that learning means just learning accepted facts. But what really interests me is using computers to transmit ideas, points of view, ways of thinking. You don't need a computer for this, but just as with a musical instrument, once you get onto this way of using them, then the computer is a great amplifier for learning."

## At-risk and high tech

For three years, beginning in 1999, I worked with Seymour Papert to develop a high-tech alternative learning environment, the Constructionist Learning Laboratory (CCL), inside the Maine Youth Center (MYC), the state facility for adjudicated teens. This multiage environment provided each student with a personal computer and access to a variety of constructive material. The experience of trying to reacquaint or acquaint these previously unsuccessful students with the learning process teaches us many lessons about just how at-risk our entire educational system has become.

The intent of the project was to create a rich constructionist learning environment in which severely at-risk students - many of whom seemed to suffer from what Papert called "the curious epidemic of learning disabilities" - could be engaged in long-term projects based on personal interest, expertise, and experience. Students used computational technologies, programmable LEGO, and more traditional materials to construct knowledge through the act of creating a personally meaningful project. The hypothesis was that the constructionist philosophy offers students better opportunities to learn and engage in personally meaningful intellectual development. The computer was the magic carpet that would allow these children to escape their history of school failure.

Several case studies from this research could be used to support the claim that constructing knowledge in a technologically rich

113

environment leads learners of all ages to view the world differently. This paradigm shift offers promise for the creation of future learning environments and in the preparation of future teachers.

Kids with low or non-existent literacy skills were able to invent and program robots capable of making decisions and interacting with their environment. Robo Sumo wrestlers, interactive gingerbread houses, card dealing robots, luggage sorting systems, and temperature-sensitive vending machines capable of charging a customer more money on hot humid days were but a few of the ingenious inventions constructed with programmable LEGO materials. Students also designed their own videogames, made movies, and explored the universe via computer-controlled microscopes and telescopes. They wrote sequels to Othello and published articles in programming journals. These kids proved that computing offered productive learning opportunities for all kinds of minds.

One child, said to be completely illiterate, wrote a page of program code the night before class because an idea was burning inside of him. Another "illiterate" youngster, incarcerated for more than half of his life, built dozens of mechanisms in the blink of an eye, and could install complex software. His ability to program complicated robots presented clues about his true abilities. A week before he left the facility, this child, so accustomed to school failure, sat down and typed a 12,000-word autobiography.

Tony's adventure is also a tale worth telling. He had not been in school since the seventh grade, and indicated that none of his peer group attended school past the age of twelve or thirteen. In the CLL, he fell in love with robotics and photography at the age of seventeen.

During the spring of 2001, the MYC campus was populated with groundhog holes. To most kids, these familiar signs of spring went unnoticed, but not for the "new" Tony.

Tony and his new assistant, Craig, spent the next few weeks building a series of what came to be known as "Gopher-cams" – LEGO robots equipped with flashlights and USB cameras tethered to a laptop computer. This work captured the imagination of the entire Maine Youth Center. Tony and Craig learned a great deal about how simple, unanticipated obstacles like a twig could derail days of planning and require new programming or engineering. These students engaged in a process of exploration not unlike that experienced by the men who sailed the high seas or landed on the moon. While they never really found out what was down the hole, they learned many much more important lessons.

Robotics gives life to engineering, mathematics, and computer science in a tactile form. It is a concrete manifestation of problem solving that rewards debugging, ingenuity and persistence. The LEGO robotic materials possess an improvisational quality that allows even young children to build a machine, test a hypothesis, tinker, debug, and exceed their own expectations. Like in programming, every incremental success leads to a larger question or the construction of a bigger theory. This dialogue with the machine amplifies and mediates a conversation with self. The LEGO contributed an improvisational quality to student thinking.

Digital technology can be a critical variable in the transformation of reluctant learners. Self-esteem, or even academic grades, might have been enhanced through traditional activities for CCL students. However, the availability of computationally-rich construction materials afforded these learners the opportunity to experience the empowerment associated with the feeling of wonderful ideas. For the first time in their lives, these children experienced what it felt like to be engaged in intellectual work. This feeling required a personal sustained relationship with the computer and computationally-rich objects to think with such as LEGO. All students deserve the chance to make important contributions to the world of ideas, and must be given the means to do so.

## State of the Art?
Much needs to be done to ensure that all students enjoy the quality of experience offered by the best laptop schools, online environments, and the CLL.

Somewhere along the line, the dreams of Kay, Papert, and Loader were diluted by the inertia of school. Detours along the road to the Dynabook were paved by the emergence of the Internet and corporate interest in the laptop miracle. Until the explosion of interest in the Internet and Web, individual laptops offered a relatively low-cost, decentralized way to increase access to computers and rich learning opportunities. The Net, however, required these machines to be tethered to centralized servers and an educational bureaucracy pleased with its newfound control. Computing costs soared; data and children were either menaced or menaces. Jobs needed to be protected. The desires of the many often trumped the needs of the learner.

Microsoft generously offered to bring the laptop message to American schools, but their promotional videos pushed desks back into rows and teachers stood at the front of classrooms directing their students to use Excel to calculate the perimeter of a rectangle. Over emphasis on clerical "business" applications were manifest in elaborate projects designed to justify the use of Excel or PowerPoint in an unchanged curriculum. Many of these projects have the dubious distinction of being mechanically impressive while educationally pointless. Our gullible embrace of false complexity increases as the work is projected in a darkened classroom.

I've developed Murray's Law to describe the way in which many schools assimilate powerful technology: Every 18 months, schools will purchase computers with twice the processing power of today, and do things twice as trivial with those computers.

There is a fundamental difference between technology and computing, which can be seen in the words themselves. One is a noun, the other a verb. What we saw students do with technology at the CCL was active, engaged, compelling, sophisticated learning. They were computing, and similar experiences for all students can transform the experience of school.

I know that many of you must be thinking, "Does Gary really believe that everyone should be a programmer?" My answer is, "No, but every child should experience the opportunity to program a computer during her K-12 education." Critics of my position will say things like, "Not every person needs to program or will even like it." To these people I suggest that not every kid needs to learn to write haiku or sand a tie rack in woodshop. However, we require millions of children to do these things because we believe it is either rewarding, of cultural value, or offers a window into potential forms of human expression.

Despite our high-tech society's infinite dependence on programming and the impressive rewards for computing innovation, many people find the notion of programming repulsive. Some educators especially need to get past this hysteria rooted in fear and ignorance for the sake of the children in our care.

I do not understand why anyone would question the value of offering programming experiences to children.

It is unseemly for schools to determine that a tiny fraction of the student population is capable of using computers in an intellectually rich way. The "drill for the test" curriculum of the A.P. Computer Science course serves only a few of the most technically sophisticated students. That is elitism.

Children enjoy programming when engaged in a supportive environment. The study of other disciplines may be enhanced through the ability to make abstract ideas concrete. It would be difficult to argue that mathematics education would not be enriched through related programming activities.

Schools need to make a sufficient number of computers with powerful software available for the transparent use of every child across all disciplines. Schools also have an obligation to offer a more inclusive selection of courses designed for a more diverse student body interested in learning with and about computers. Courses in software design, digital communication, robotics, or computer science are but a few options. The Generation Y program, in which students lend their technological expertise to teachers who want to integrate technology into their lessons, provides another outlet for authentic practice.

**Whither Computing?**
I wonder when the educational computing community decided to replace the word. computing, with technology? The Computing Teacher became Learning and Leading with Technology, Classroom Computer Learning begot Technology and Learning Magazine. Conference speakers began diminishing the power of the computer by lumping all sorts of objects into the catch-all of technology. Computers are in fact a technology, but they are now spoken of in the same breath as the blackboard, chalk, filmstrip projector or Waterpik. Computing was never to be mentioned again in polite company.

I recently read the conference program for a 1985 educational computing conference. The topics of discussion and sessions offered are virtually the same as at similar events today. The only difference is that all mentions of programming have disappeared from the marketplace of ideas.

It seems ironic that educators fond of reciting how kids know so much about computers act as if the computer was just invented. Increasingly schools view children of the digital age as either potential victims or potential felons. Many policymakers seem to believe the combination of youth and silicon will spawn evil little villains or victims of Belarusian pedophiles. I suspect that subscribing to neither extreme is constructive.

The best way to keep children from using computers in destructive ways is to engage them in constructive pursuits. If the dominant use of computers is for looking up information, then it should come as no surprise that kids look up inappropriate stuff. The over-reliance on computers as information appliances allows idle minds to get in trouble.

We should be unimpressed by breathless tales of children Web surfing or using a word processor to write a school report. My standards are much higher. We will cheat a second generation of microcomputer-age students if we do not raise our game and acknowledge that so much more is possible.

If we stipulate that kids are at least comfortable with computers, if not fluent, then teachers have a responsibility to build on the fluency of computer-savvy kids. This is a classroom gift, like an early reader, a natural soprano, or a six year-old dinosaur expert. It is incumbent on schools and their personnel to steer such students in more challenging and productive directions. Teachers have an obligation to respect the talents, experience and knowledge of students by creating authentic opportunities for growth.

If the youngest children can "play" doctor, lawyer, teacher, or fireman, let's add software designer to the list. Open-ended software construction environments designed for children, like LEGO and MicroWorlds, make it possible for children of all ages to view themselves as competent and creative producers of knowledge. Too few students know that such accomplishments are within reach. This failure results from a leadership, vision, and professional knowledge deficit.

While school computing fades from memory, keyboarding instruction inexplicably remains a K-12 staple from coast to coast. Computer assisted instruction, schemes designed to reduce reading to a high-stakes race and low-level technical skills dominate the use of computers in schools. In the hands of a clever curriculum committee, "uses scroll bars" can be part of a nine-year scope and sequence. Examples of kids composing music, constructing robots, or designing their own simulations are too hard to find. More than a quarter century has passed since Mr. Jones taught me to program. It's way past time to include all children in the joy of exploration and mastery I felt. Yet, children in that school are now compelled to complete a keyboarding class. There can be no rational justification for so blatant a dumbing-down of the curriculum.

## Computing Changes Everything
There are so many ways in which children may use computers in authentic ways. Low-cost MIDI software and hardware offers even young children a vehicle for musical composition. The 1990 NCTM Standards indicated that fifty percent of mathematics has been invented since World War II. This mathematics is visual, experimental and rooted in computing. It may even engage kids in the beauty, function and magic of mathematics.

In *Seeing in the Dark: How Backyard Stargazers Are Probing Deep Space and Guarding Earth from Interplanetary Peril*, author Timothy Ferris describes how amateur astronomers armed with telescopes, computers and Net connections are making substantive contributions to the field of astronomy. For the first time in history, children possess the necessary tools to be scientists and to engage in scientific communities.

MacArthur Genius Stephen Wolfram has written a revolutionary new 1,280 page book, *A New Kind of Science*. The book illustrates his theory that the universe and countless other disciplines may be reduced to a simple algorithm. Scientists agree that if just a few percent of Wolfram's theories are true, much of what we thought we knew could be wrong and many other cosmic mysteries may be solved. Wolfram believes that a human being is no more intelligent than a cloud and both may be created with a simple computer program.

*A New Kind of Science* starts with very a big bang.

"Three centuries ago science was transformed by the dramatic new idea that rules based on mathematical equations could be used to describe the natural world. My purpose in this book is to initiate another such transformation, and to introduce a new kind of science that is based on the much more general types of rules that can be embodied in simple computer programs."

You do not have to take Wolfram's word for it. With the $65 *A New Kind of Science Explorer* software, you and your students can explore more than 450 of Wolfram's experiments. The visual nature of cellular automata - the marriage of science, computer graphics and mathematics - allows children to play on the frontiers of scientific thought while trying to prove, disprove or extend the theories of one of the world's greatest scientists. The intellectual habits required to "think with" this tool are rooted in computer programming.

I recently told Alan Kay that while I was hardly a mathematician, I knew what it felt like to have a mathematical idea. He generously replied, "Then you are a mathematician, you're just not a professional." The work of Seymour Papert shows us that the computer allows children to be mathematicians and scientists.

"If you can use technology to make things you can make a lot more interesting things. And you can learn a lot more by making them. ...We are entering a digital world where knowing about digital technology is as important as reading and writing. So learning about computers is essential for our students' futures BUT the most important purpose is using them NOW to learn about everything else. " (Papert 1999)

We can neutralize our critics and improve the lives of kids if we shift our focus towards using school computers for the purpose of constructing knowledge through the explicit act of making things, including robots, music compositions, digital movies, streaming radio, and simulations. Children engaged in thoughtful projects might impress citizens desperate for academic rigor. Examples of competent children computing bring many current educational practices into question. Emphasizing the use of computers to make things will make life easier for teachers, more exciting for learners and lead schools into what should be education's golden age.

### Epilogue: Why Should Schools Compute?
*Computing offers an authentic context for doing and making mathematics*
Traditional arithmetic and mathematical processes are provided with a genuine context for use. New forms of mathematics become accessible to learners.

*Computing concretizes the abstract*
Formal concepts like feedback, variables and causality become concrete through use.

*Computing offers new avenues for creative expression*
Computing makes forms of visual art and music composition possible for even young children while providing a canvas for the exploration of new art forms like animation. A limitless audience is now possible.

*Computer science is a legitimate science*
Computer science plays a revolutionary role in society and in every other science. It should be studied alongside biology, physics and chemistry.

*Computing supports a plurality of learning styles*
There are many ways to approach a problem and express a solution.

*Computing offers preparation for a plethora of careers*
There is a shortage of competent high-tech professionals in our economy

*Computing gives agency to the user, not the computer*
Rather than the computer programming the child, the child can control the computer.

*Debugging offers ongoing opportunities to enhance problem-solving skills*
Nothing works correctly the first time. The immediacy of concrete feedback makes debugging a skill that will serve learners for a lifetime.

*Computing rewards habits of mind such as persistence, curiosity and perspective*

Computers mediate a conversation with self in which constant feedback and incremental success propels learners to achieve beyond their expectations.

## References

Cavallo, D. (1999) "Project Lighthouse in Thailand: Guiding Pathways to Powerful Learning." In *Logo Philosophy and Implementation*. Montreal, Canada: LCSI.

Duckworth, E. (1996) *The Having of Wonderful Ideas and Other Essays on Teaching and Learning*. NY: Teachers College Press.

Ferris, T. (2002) *Seeing in the Dark: How Backyard Stargazers Are Probing Deep Space and Guarding Earth from Interplanetary Peril*. NY: Simon and Schuster.

Harel, I., and Papert, S., eds. (1991) *Constructionism*. Norwood, NJ: Ablex Publishing.

Kafai, Y., and Resnick, M., eds. (1996) *Constructionism in Practice: Designing, Thinking, and Learning in a Digital World*. Mahwah, NJ: Lawrence Erlbaum.

Kay, Alan (2003) "The Dynabook Revisted" from the website, *The Book and the Computer: exploring the future of the printed word in the digital age*. (n.d.) Retrieved January 20, 2003 from http://www.honco.net/os/kay.html.

Levy, S. (2002) The Man Who Cracked the Code to Everything. *Wired Magazine*. Volume 10, Issue 6. June 2002.

Papert, S. (1980) *Mindstorms: Children, Computers, and Powerful Ideas*. New York: Basic Books.

Papert, S. (1990) "A Critique of Technocentrism in Thinking About the School of the Future," *MIT Epistemology and Learning Memo No. 2*. Cambridge, Massachusetts: Massachusetts Institute of Technology Media Laboratory.

Papert, S. (1991) "Situating Constructionism." In *Constructionism*, in Harel, I., and Papert, S., eds. Norwood, NJ: Ablex Publishing.

Papert, S. (1993) *The Children's Machine: Rethinking School in the Age of the Computer*. New York: Basic Books.

Papert, S. (1996) *The Connected Family*. Atlanta: Longstreet Publishing.

Papert, S. (1999) "The Eight Big Ideas of the Constructionist Learning Laboratory." Unpublished internal document. South Portland, Maine.

Papert, S. (1999) "What is Logo? Who Needs it?" In *Logo Philosophy and Implementation*. Montreal, Canada: LCSI.

Papert, S. (2000) "What's the Big Idea? Steps toward a pedagogy of idea power." *IBM Systems Journal*, Vol. 39, Nos 3&4, 2000.

Resnick, M., and Ocko, S. (1991) "LEGO/Logo: Learning Through and About Design." In *Constructionism*, in Harel, I., and Papert, S., eds. Norwood, NJ: Ablex Publishing.

Stager, G. (2001) "Computationally-Rich Constructionism and At-Risk Learners." Presented at the World Conference on Computers in Education. Copenhagen.

Stager, G. (2002) "Papertian Constructionism and At-Risk Learners." Presented at the National Educational Computing Conference. San Antonio.

Turkle, S. (1991) *"Epistemological Pluralism and the Revaluation of the Concrete." In Constructionism*. Idit Harel and Seymour Papert (eds.), Norwood, NJ: Ablex Publishing.

Wolfram, S. (2002) *A New Kind of Science*. Champaign, IL: Wolfram Media, Inc.

# From Data to Understanding:
## Navigating Informational Spaces in the Age of Overwhelm

David D. Thornburg, Ph.D.
tcpd2020@aol.com

*The material in this chapter is excerpted from presentations and workshops on this topic created and presented by the author to educators at all levels. A full book expanding on the topic of this chapter is in progress.*

*The challenge:*

The first half of the twentieth century was filled with remarkable inventions: radio, television, airplanes, the computer. Most of the marvels we take for granted were already well-established by 1950. While the second half of the twentieth century had its contributions as well – cable TV, the personal computer, wireless devices (pagers, cell phones, PDA's), and the Internet, to name just a few, these were largely refinements of ideas that were already known by 1950. Even the hypertext underpinnings of the Web were published in a popular magazine by 1945 (Bush, 1945).

The biggest changes that took place in the last 50 years of the twentieth century dealt with our relationships to information, not the invention of the information-handling tools themselves. For example, information flow in corporations in the 1950's was largely the same as that found in the 1890's. The flattening of hierarchies in companies that came with the rise of distributed information access was a phenomenon of the last 50 years. In addition to differences in the ways we handled information, the last half of the twentieth century gave us ever more information to deal with. Compared with the early years of the century, the speed and volume of information exchange grew to staggering proportions.

The virtual deluge of data from all sources today threatens to drown us all. Some commentators on the current scene, like Richard Saul Wurman (Wurman, 2001), point out that the daily *New York Times* has more information than an average person would be exposed to during a lifetime in 17th century England. We are at the point where every institution, including our schools, has entered a new age with regard to information access and management.

Not only have our traditional forms of information grown in size, we live in an era where the new media do not displace old ones, but simply provide additional sources of information added to our overflowing supply. We live in the "Age of Also" (Wurman, 2001). To see this, compare media use for 1996 and 2003 (projected) shown in Table 1 (from *Statistical Abstracts of the United States*, 2003)

**Hours Per Person Per Year (U. S.)**

|                    | 1996  | 2003  |
|--------------------|-------|-------|
| Television         | 1,559 | 1,649 |
| Radio              | 973   | 990   |
| Recorded music     | 292   | 246   |
| Daily newspapers   | 162   | 146   |
| Popular magazines  | 112   | 103   |
| Consumer books     | 100   | 88    |
| Home video         | 54    | 70    |
| Video games        | 25    | 97    |
| Box office         | 12    | 12    |
| Home Internet      | 10    | 182   |
| **Total**          | **3,297** | **3,583** |

Table 1. Hours spent exploring information

With the exception of recorded music and print media, the number of hours people spend exposed to information has grown in most categories, in some cases remarkably. For example, contrary to popular opinion, television use did not decline as a result of the World Wide Web. Rather than trade off one informational form for another, we seem to be increasing the total time spent in the pursuit of information. When you consider that we only spend 2,000 hours per year at work (assuming 50 forty-hour work weeks per year), the time we spend in pursuit of information in all its forms is staggering.

As for the sheer volume of information available to people, Peter Lyman and Hal Varian and their colleagues at Berkeley have shown that the world's total yearly production of print, film, optical, and magnetic content would require roughly 1.5 billion gigabytes of storage. This is the equivalent of 250 megabytes per person for each man, woman, and child on earth (Lyman and Varian, 2001). To put this number in human terms, the annual production of data would require each person on the planet to have about 3 meters of shelf space to hold all this data, assuming it was in printed form.

We share ideas and information with colleagues in an increasingly wireless society. While US Census data showed only 5.3 million cell phone users in 1990, that number jumped to 109.5 million in 2001. When not on the phone, it seems that many of us have cameras in our hands as we hurriedly snap some 80 billion photographs each year (Lyman and Varian, 2001).

Internet access is increasing, even during the "dot com" collapse. Nielsen Netratings (2003) found that broadband access jumped 59% to 33.6 million users in December of 2002, with 74.4 million users still using dial-up access. They found that the average home/work user visits 1336 Web pages and spends 45 hours per month online. This scarcely leaves time to read the 96,000 books, 14,000 magazines and 11,000 newspapers published every year (*Statistical Abstracts of the United States*, 2003).

As for e-mail, in 2000, 81 million Americans sent 2.1 billion personal and business messages per day, with advertisers sending an additional 7.3 billion. During that year the US Postal Service delivered 107 billion pieces of 1st class mail. This means that there were over 30 e-mails for every piece of first class mail, a trend that is growing rapidly.

There is no question that we are overwhelmed with information, or, more accurately, overwhelmed with faceless data flooding us from every quarter.

Even web sites designed to help educators and students can be pretty intimidating. For example, the excellent resources listed by the U. S. Department of Education's "Free" site (www.ed.gov/ free) provide links to an overwhelming number of resources including (as of March 2003):

400 art sites,
50 educational technology sites,
50 foreign language sites,
110 health and safety sites,
160 language arts sites,
50 math sites,
6 physical education sites,
570 science sites,
800 social studies sites, and,
20 vocational education sites.

Furthermore, many of the referenced sites contain incredibly large libraries of information related to their subject area.


*The fractal nature of information*
A student doing Web-based research on just about any topic gets to experience the fractal nature of information. Fractals are mathematical objects whose complexity does not diminish as they are magnified. In some cases, the apparent complexity even increases.

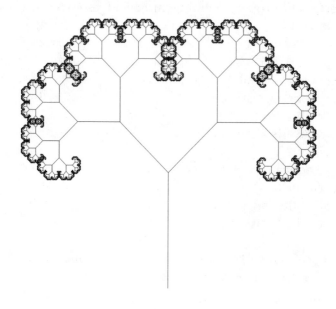

Figure 1. A fractal information tree in which each node represents a data resource that leads to two others. At six levels deep the pattern becomes quite complex.

This aspect of searching for information in a hypertext environment was understood clearly by Vannevar Bush, the inventor of the concept of hypertext, in his classic 1945 article, *As We May Think*, published in the Atlantic Monthly. In this article he described a device called a "memex" that we can think of as a personal computer connected to the Web. His description of exploration in this environment is amazingly accurate:

> The owner of the memex, let us say, is interested in the origin and properties of the bow and arrow. Specifically he

is studying why the short Turkish bow was apparently superior to the English long bow in the skirmishes of the Crusades. He has dozens of possibly pertinent books and articles in his memex. First he runs through an encyclopedia, finds an interesting but sketchy article, leaves it projected. Next, in a history, he finds another pertinent item, and ties the two together. Thus he goes, building a trail of many items. Occasionally he inserts a comment of his own, either linking it into the main trail or joining it by a side trail to a particular item. When it becomes evident that the elastic properties of available materials had a great deal to do with the bow, he branches off on a side trail which takes him through textbooks on elasticity and tables of physical constants. He inserts a page of longhand analysis of his own. Thus he builds a trail of his interest through the maze of materials available to him.

The rule of the Web is simple: the more you dig the more you find, and the richer the branches become. Instead of running out of information, you are linked into ever more complex threads. For example, someone researching the Blues would immediately find links to music, geography, and history (not to mention blue jeans and other topics off the main subject of the search). Digging deeper, topics such as race relations, prisons, the economy, rock and roll, jazz, and social commentary come into view – and on and on it goes. The well never runs dry.

*Learning at the edge of chaos*
Educators interested in addressing this challenge might suggest going back to the simpler days of a textbook-driven curriculum. After all, when we relied on textbooks, the content was clearly defined and crafted so as to be approachable and appropriate for specific grades and subjects. The world of the textbook is, compared with the chaos of the Web, quite tidy.

Textbooks have several attributes:

1.  They close doors to information, presenting only what others have deemed important.
2.  They are written by experts who can be counted on to define the "proper" scope and sequence of information. (Think, for example, of E. D. Hirsch's efforts on Cultural Literacy)
3.  They offer a finite and rigidly defined curriculum, ignoring the fact that order is no guarantee of understanding.
4.  They are replenished by schools only after many years of use (eight years, for example), by which time much of their content has become outdated.

While some of the surface challenges created in the Age of Overwhelm can be overcome through a return to the instructional practices of the past, the old textbook model appears misguided for several reasons. First, if confined to a textbook-driven education, once students leave school they will spend the rest of their lives in a world where they are deluged with data they have no idea how to handle. Second, "understanding" (as I'll explore later) is not the same as knowledge. Understanding is highly personal, and the path to understanding must be traversed by each learner in his or her own way, not dictated by the understandings of a textbook author whose prose is dictated by faceless committees.

Years ago we used to say, "Content is king." Today we are drowning in content, opening the question to what reigns today. Is context king? How about communication, or connection, or creativity, or combinations of all these? Clearly, context is important because it provides the framework in which content can be placed and where real learning can happen. Communication, a highly human trait, is the means through which ideas can be shared and

134

meaning found. Connection between ideas, the linkages that build deep understanding, is also important, as is the creativity with which we use current knowledge as a springboard to new discoveries. When viewed in this context, there is no one clear winner – all the potential kings are important, as are some not yet identified.

Let's assume for the moment that one of the goals of education is understanding. How do we create environments that build understanding in students? The path moves from data, to information, to knowledge, and then to understanding, and (if we are lucky) from there to wisdom.

As described in a sidebar commentary by Nathan Shedroff in *Information Anxiety 2* (Wurman, 2001), data involves research, creation, gathering, and discovery. Information involves presentation and organization. Knowledge involves conversations, storytelling, and integration. Understanding involves evaluation, interpretation, and retrospection. As we go from data to understanding we move from the completely impersonal to the highly personal and from content to context. But even if we accept these aspects of data, information, knowledge, and understanding, we are no closer to knowing how to move from one level to the next. (Actually, Shedroff uses the term "wisdom" instead of "understanding," a distinction we will explore later.)

*The Care and Feeding of Trees*
Any home gardener knows that healthy trees need both to grow and to be pruned. I think the same is true of learning. We need to grow our knowledge, but at the same time must learn to prune those branches we come across that divert us from our goal. This does not mean that side branches are not interesting – in fact they might provide the cuttings we need to grow a new field of study. The point is that when a student is asked to research a topic for a project

(for example), the fractal nature of information insures that any interesting search is likely to sprout branches into interesting areas that might move too far away from the focus of the project at hand. The critical concept here is the incremental cost of ignorance. While it is possible that further research will unearth even more relevant information on a topic, at some point the researcher needs to stop collecting data and start working with what has already been found.

In other words, just as it is essential to know how organize a search to locate and organize data, it is important to know what data streams to leave behind on the road to understanding. This is a non-trivial process for several reasons, not the least of which is that some of the new branches may point the way to research projects far more interesting than the one the student started out exploring. And, that elusive tidbit might just be one mouse-click away. As hard as it may be, there comes a time when you need to let the bits go.

One approach to developing a sense of what data is important is to build an outline of the final project. Unfortunately, outlines often require a clear mental map of the scope of the subject being explored. Most of us experienced this challenge when we were students. In fact, the only way I could create an outline for a research paper was to write the paper first, and then build the outline from the first draft of the final project. I agree with W. H. Auden when he said, "We do not write to express what we know, but to discover what we are thinking."

The problem is amplified today in the data deluge that springs onto our computer screens in response to almost any Web search.

*The role of technology*
Since the telematic technology of Internet-connected computers helps get us into this mess, it is appropriate to ask if it can also help us get out of it. I think it can.

Because much of what follows is summarized in the diagram shown in Figure 2, you might want to have a copy of this figure in front of you as proceed. This diagram is centered on the movement from Data (D) to Information (I) to Knowledge (K) to Understanding (U).

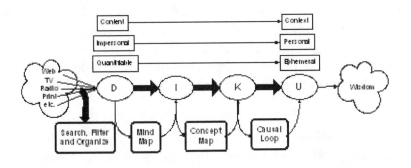

Figure 2. From Data to Understanding

At the left edge we have the cloud of raw data in all of its forms. This includes (but is not limited to) the huge repositories of all the Web sites on the planet, all the books in all the libraries, and every piece of information broadcast in any form on any station. From here we move to Data (D), by which I mean the specific data sets germane to a student research topic or project. This collection of data is the result of organized searches and a filtering process by the researcher to limit the volume of accumulated tidbits to those that relate to the topic being explored. Data leads to Information (I), which leads to Knowledge (K), and this leads to Understanding (U), a proper goal for education. Beyond Understanding lies Wisdom – an ultimate goal that, depending on its definition, can take a lifetime to achieve.

As we move from left to right on this diagram, we move from content to context, from the realm of the highly impersonal (Data)

137

to the highly personal (Understanding), and from the readily quantifiable to the more ephemeral.

The first challenge any learner encounters when conducting a project that has already been defined is to locate and organize relevant data from a variety of sources. As much data as can be found on the Internet, it likely represents only a fraction of the data germane to the topic being explored. The critical issues are not completeness but usability. If the data set is sufficiently broad, it is likely that it can form the raw material that will lead, ultimately, to understanding.

But how does one proceed? Using the Web as an example, search tools like **Google** come to mind. But whether one uses **Google**, **Alta Vista**, or any of the myriad search tools available, the results of the search will include references that are irrelevant and those that are inaccurate. So the first task is for learners to learn how to distinguish the useful and accurate from the spurious and false – to evaluate resources. This foundational skill is essential for all of us, and especially for our youth. No matter how proficient they are at using the Web, they will not know how to address this issue without some guidance. Librarians spend a long time developing these skills, and these skills get refined with practice.

In fact, even the best Web search tools are fine for specific inquiries (what is the ZIP code for Lake Barrington?), but are troublesome when exploring domains of inquiry (What resources explore the topic of Civil Rights?) The problem arises from the fact that search engines do not organize their results in a contextual manner. This challenge is elegantly addressed with a tool called **Grokker** that builds a contextual map of a search through the use of metadata. This map organizes related Web sites into broader categories and allows the entire dataspace related to your query to be displayed on one screen. Furthermore, once a Grokker map has been constructed, it can be explored off-line allowing the researcher to choose the sites that warrant close inspection and organize them into a special group to be examined the next time the user goes online.

In the absence of tools to organize search results, many students simply grab onto the first search result they find, often missing far better resources that lay buried in an immense number of proposed sites.

Tools for further organizing data can depend on the form the data takes. Textual information can be stored as text files or inside a database. Images can be organized and catalogued using image management tools such as **ACDSee**, or **Photoshop Album** by Adobe. The key to a good tool is its ability to let you locate specific results of your research quickly.

Once a relevant and (presumably) accurate collection of data is found and organized the learner is ready to convert this data into information. The difference between data and information is organization and connections. Tools like Mind Mapping are very powerful in this context. A central idea representing the project is surrounded by branching trees of data whose structure shows the connections between data and their relationship to the central theme of the project. **Inspiration** is the most common software used for building mind maps or conceptual webs. The process of building a map often highlights areas where the data is weak, and also points to directions for future research.

The move from information to knowledge builds beyond the identification of links between different pieces of data. The relationships between pieces of information define knowledge. For example, you might know that many plants have roots, stems, leaves, flowers and seeds, and that green plants need nutrients, water and light. But with all this information there is no evidence of knowledge. It is the integration of this information that leads to knowledge. If information is built from the nouns of data, knowledge is built by connecting these nouns with verbs.

A powerful tool for building and representing this level of knowledge is called Concept Mapping in which concepts are provided with a context. At first glance a concept map looks similar to a mind map or web. The primary difference is that each of the links connecting informational segments now contains a verb or verb phrase that defines the relationship between these two pieces of information. Words like photosynthesis, leaves, light, nutrients, and energy take on new meaning when they are connected with the relevant verbs that describe their relationships.

Again, the program **Inspiration** is well-suited for this task, allowing concept maps to be built with ease.

While knowledge is great to have (and represents the bulk of what is measured on tests we give our students), it is not the same as understanding. To understand something is to be able to interpret it, to truly make it our own, and to transfer, apply and explore connections between the things we know, even if they represent knowledge from different disciplines.

There are many paths to understanding. One that relates somewhat to mind maps and concept maps is called the Causal Loop Diagram. These diagrams, common to the exploration of systems, not only identify the relationships between objects or concepts, they explore the deeper issues of causality and even allow the examination of feedback loops where one parameter can influence a second, which can influence a third, which can then influence the first one. These loops, common in the real world, cannot be modeled using spreadsheets but can be explored in depth using computer tools like **Stella** or the far easier program **Model-It**. Simulations of complex systems built with these programs can be operated and, as variables are changed, the user can see the response of the whole system.

While it may seem that causal mapping applies to readily quantifiable domains (such as engineering projects), it applies to the study of history or literature as well. Causal loops let you explore "What if?" questions that lead to deeper and deeper understanding of the subject of your exploration.

Without doubt we are living in a world of immense complexity. The challenge felt by educator and learner alike is to avoid being swamped by the rising tide of data as we ride the crest of the wave toward understanding. While we are powerless to stem the tide of discovery and expression, we do have the power to help others learn how to make meaning from the overload that inundates us daily – to move from data to understanding.

*Resources for data and information*
American Memory Project, www.loc.gov
Earth images, earthobservatory.nasa.gov
Educational resources (non-commercial), www.ed.gov/free
Space images, www.nasa.gov
Weather images, www.noaa.gov

*Resources for tools*
ACDSee image management software: www.acdsystems.com
Grokker: www.groxis.com
Inspiration: www.inspiration.com
Model-It: www.goknow.com
Photoshop Album: www.adobe.com
Stella: www.hps-inc.com

*Other resources:*
Burmark, Lynell (2002) *Visual Literacy*, ASCD.

Bush, Vannevar (1945) *As We May Think,* **Atlantic Monthly,** July,(www.theatlantic.com/unbound/flashbks/computer/bu shf.htm)

Center for Media Education, *Teensites.com,* www.cme.org

Hirsch, E. D., *et al.* (2002) *The New Dictionary of Cultural Literacy,* Houghton Mifflin.

Lenhart, Amanda, Rainie, Lee , and Lewis, Oliver (2001) *Teenage life online: The rise of the instant-message generation and the Internet's impact on friendships and family relationships,* Pew Internet and American Life project, www.pewinternet.org

Lyman, Peter and Varian, Hal (2001) *How Much Information?,* www.sims.berkeley.edu/how-much-info/

National Academy of Engineering, *Greatest Engineering Accomplishments of the 20th Century,* www.greatachievements.org

Nielsen Netratings (2003) www.nielsen-netratings.com

U. S. Department of Commerce, *Statistical Abstracts of the United States,* www.census.gov/statab/www/

Wurman, Richard Saul (2001) *Information Anxiety 2,* QUE.

# Media Perspectives on Student Understanding:
## A National Talent Search Contest for Students-at-Work

*Hosted by: North Central Regional Technology in Education Consortium at North Central Regional Educational Lab (NCRTEC at NCREL), The Thornburg Center for Professional Development (TCPD), Bernajean Porter Consulting*

### Introduction:

Students across our nation's classrooms are embracing multimedia and Web tools to give even more power to their communication skills. A new challenge has come to our classrooms as national studies and organizations work to define 21$^{st}$ Century Skills (http://www.ncrel.org/engauge/skills/ indepth.htm) deemed essential for students to thrive in a digital economy. Student work or products have traditionally been produced in response to a teacher's request to "go look up and tell me back" so students can demonstrate they are good consumers of information. A true knowledge-building environment facilitates inquiry research. This enables learning to be centered on key ideas, deeper levels of understanding, and original thinking that goes beyond existing information, rather than the completion of often unrelated activities. Meeting the new 21$^{st}$ Century Skills demand will require shifting student work into higher gear from activities that use knowledge to activities that practice skills focused on students being information seekers, analyzers, evaluators, innovative thinkers, problem-solvers, decision makers, and finally producers of knowledge that was gained in the process.

The new skills create an urgent demand on learners to acquire and practice the higher order thinking skills from the top of Bloom's Taxonomy - analyzing, synthesizing, and evaluating. We are not concerned only with creating and assessing student computer-based products but about also, more importantly, with the opportunity to increase overall student performance by reorganizing classroom life to be environments of sustained inquiry, cognitive apprenticeships, authentic work, and where original thinking is produced. Since students need to do some kind of work in order to learn, why not let that work be the construction of knowledge?

Evaluating student computer-based products is about assessing the effective communication of content knowledge that is useful and beneficial to others. Student scoring guides were created to assess student computer-based products. They were intentionally designed to help set and raise the quality bar of student work to perhaps even go beyond local expectations of teachers and schools. Many student products will not score well on the student scoring guides because the purpose of the student assignment used technology for its own sake, or lacked expectations/guidance for students to create knowledge products. Knowledge building is not just being the first person to develop a new, previously unknown idea. An original theory or explanation is only one kind of knowledge product. Other worthwhile products of knowledge-building are interpretations of theories, criticisms, translations of complex ideas into simpler terms, analyses of implications or applications, descriptions of phenomena which the theory does or does not explain, experimental demonstrations, simulations, historical accounts, and so on. (Bereiter, 1996)

As important as learning and knowing is in schools, it is not enough - learners also need to acquire exemplary skills in communicating or demonstrating to others their deep understanding of ideas and concepts. Students' expertise is valued by becoming community property in the form of a knowledge product. With the exponential growth of information, we can no longer rely only upon our own individual learning. Learning communities allow for the sharing of expertise, thereby increasing our own capacity to deal with the explosion of information in meaningful ways.

We have found there are two challenges when students use various media for expression. First, most students have not had extensive education in these expressive forms, and, as a consequence, their projects fail to make effective use of the chosen media. Second, many educators need help in learning how to assess student computer-based work. Teachers need preparation to go beyond the technology to assess both the content and the use of the chosen media in communicating the topic - focusing the evaluation on whether the student work demonstrates both mastery and clarity of understanding useful and beneficial to others.

We have decided to address these challenges by organizing a national contest to encourage students and teachers in using media to express deep understanding of ideas and concepts.

This contest highlights the use of special assessment scoring guides based on national benchmarks and studies geared to the needs of educators to effectively measure the quality of student computer-based products.

The contest has two goals. First, to reward and honor exemplary work by students and teachers, and second, to bring national attention to assessment tools teachers presently have access to online that effectively increase the quality of student computer-based projects.

## Purposes:
1. To demonstrate the ability of media to provide various lens through which students can communicate their expression of deep understanding in any content area
2. To disseminate understanding and use of assessment tools presently available to all educators - tools that focus student work on demonstrating understanding of ideas / concepts, not simply using technology for its own sake
3. To generate exemplary examples of students' capacity to create and communicate their expertise as models for teachers to use in examining future student work
4. To generate examples of teacher lessons demonstrating exemplary environments for students to express deep understanding in a content area
5. To create motivational environments that support a joy of learning

## Scoring Tools
The BIG question is not whether students are using technology but rather to ask what knowledge and deep understanding(s) are being demonstrated by the student's product. Student scoring guides based on fourteen types of communication were developed, benchmarked against national standards and research studies, and finally field-tested for two years by Bernajean Porter Consulting in partnership with NCRTEC at NCREL. Like the use of six trait scoring to support quality writing by all students, these student scoring guides provide the same support for developing quality communication products using all types of media. These

comprehensive tools and processes not only help us to assess individual student learning/understanding, but also provide a structure for teachers and students to shift the quality of their work into higher gear. The student scoring guide tools are presently online and available for all teachers and students for their personal use (http://www.ncrtec.org/tl/sgsp/ index.html). There are scoring guides for each of the fourteen types of communication which also provides the categories for the contest submissions.

**Types of Scoring Guides**

| Narrative | Information/ Expository | Persuasive | Environment |
|---|---|---|---|
| Personal expression | Summary reports | Advertise-ments | Participatory Environment |
| Myths/folk tales | Book reports | Describe/ conclude | |
| Short story | How-to directions | Analyze/ conclude | |
| | Biographies | Analyze/ persuade | |
| | | Compare/ contrast | |
| | | Cause/ effect | |

**Book Resource**
In addition to the online assessment tools, Bernajean Porter also developed training and resource materials for teachers to increase understanding and use of these scoring guides (Porter, 2003).

## Contest Organization

Three student categories, as well as one for teachers, will be created for each of the fourteen types of communication explored in the scoring guides. Student submission categories for student products demonstrating deep understanding of any content area include grades 3-5, grades 6-9, and grades 10-12. Student products (plus documentation) will be submitted by grade area for one of the fourteen types of communication , resulting in forty-two (14 types of communication times three grade areas) winning students. There will also be one teacher category inviting exemplary lesson design for students to express deep understanding (plus documentation of implementation results) for each of the fourteen types of communication , resulting in fourteen winning teachers. A "celebrity scoring team" will select a single GRAND prize from each of the three student grade areas and the teacher category, resulting in GRAND prizes for three students and one teacher. Sixty winning student/teacher exemplary works will be generated as models to guide future student work in our classrooms. Note: Teams of students and teachers may submit a single entry - prizes will be calculated to award to multiple team members.

Since we all are working to increase the quality of student work as well as extend the evaluation of technology's impact, this contest - assessment of meaningful student work -will provide opportunities for students and teachers to explore varied media perspectives on students' deep understanding of ideas and concepts that builds beyond existing knowledge. We look forward to sharing the exemplary communication models and hope you will join us in learning from our children.

# TIMELINE

| | |
|---|---|
| June, 2003 | Contest Launch |
| Jan 31, 2004 | Project submission deadline |
| March, 2004 | Scoring completed |
| | Final contest winners nominated |
| | Celebrity Scoring Panel selects Grand Prize Winners |
| April 1, 2004 | Winners notified |
| | Winning student products posted |
| | Winning teacher lessons posted |
| May/June, 2004 | Prizes delivered |
| June, 2004 | Grand winners announced at NECC Plenary Session |
| | Special Student Poster Session for Contest |
| | Special sessions sharing contest work / experience |
| | Launching of next year's contest |

For more information, resources, and registration packets, visit the NCRTEC at NCREL Web site (http://www.ncrtec.org). Workshops to support staff development for entries on the topics of *Data to Understanding*, *Digital Storytelling*, *Visual Literacy*, and *Raising the Bar for Student Achievement: Using Student Scoring Guides* are also available through the NCRTEC at NCREL Web site.

## References:

Bereiter, C. and Scardamalia, M. (1996). "Rethinking learning." In D.O. & N. Torrance (Eds.), *Handbook of Education and Human Development: New Models of Learning, Teaching, and Schooling* (pp. 485-513). Cambridge: MA: Basil Blackwell.

Porter, Bernajean (2003). *Evaluating Student Computer-based Products: Training and Resource Tools for Effectively Using Scoring Guides* [bjpconsulting.com]